The B
Great Commission Lifestyle

God Sent
Me Tulips

Cheri Holcomb

God Sent Me Tulips
Cheri Holcomb

Book cover and interior design by Becky Hawley Design, LLC

ISBN: 978-0-9817335-7-9

Printed in the United States of America

Published by IMD Press
7140 Hooker Street
Westminster, CO 80030
www.imdpress.com

Acknowledgements

I have to thank my "Papaw in the faith," Brother Herb Hodges of Spiritual Life Ministries. I so love and appreciate Herb and his precious wife, Judy, for all they have meant to my life personally. Had it not been for Brother Herb and his investment in my life this book would not have been possible. Much of what you will read is certainly a "tupos," a definite imprint, and a reflection of his investment through teaching and training in the Word of God. As my former pastor friend and disciple-maker, Herb has taught both my husband, Lee, and me what it means to be *others* focused. Herb is a self-less man, always focused on helping to build and train world-visionary, world-impacting disciples for Jesus Christ. As you read, I hope you can see this imprint or a clear reflection of his personal ministry in my life and my own ministry of teaching and training in the biblical principles of disciple making. This is one means of fulfilling my part in the Great Commission mandated by our Lord (Matthew 28:19-20; 2 Timothy 2:2).

There are those personal Timothys or Timothias that I must thank. These are precious sisters who have come alongside me to sharpen me, to challenge me, and most of all to support me in this ministry. God has indeed blessed me with godly partners in the faith. As I look back over the past several years of my life and ministry, I am humbled and grateful to see a ministry of multiplication through this Great Commission lifestyle of disciple making. This stuff works!

Another woman I must thank is my Aunt Lavelle, whom I affectionately call Annie. I have learned much about an intimate relationship with the Lord Jesus from this dear saint. Through her own simplistic way she has taught me much about the power of a bold witness for Christ, the privilege of prayer and the wonder of true worship. Spending time together was always, as Annie calls it, "making memories." Now residing in a nursing home, Annie is still teaching me what it means to trust Jesus. Her investment in my life has truly helped to shape my spiritual heart. I pray that I might leave a mark on others as impressionable as my Annie has left on me.

A final thanks to my precious husband, Lee. What a wonderful godly spiritual leader. He is a constant encourager for my life and ministry, and I would not want to pursue a day in the life without him. The man still melts my butter!

Forward

If you have taken this book in hand to read it, this likely means either that you are a disciple-maker who wants to re-stoke his or her fire, or a serious disciple who wants to examine the process of disciple making for yourself, or you were captivated by the colorful title, or you are just a friend of the author or one of her disciples. In any case, get ready for a quiet ambush! Cheri's testimonies and those of her disciples on these pages are genuine and true testimonies of lives revolutionized by *being* Jesus' disciples and by pursuing His mandate to build other disciples of the same kind. Cheri Holcomb is the finest female disciple maker I have ever known, and her disciples are emerging in large numbers "after the same kind." After all, did Jesus not clearly say "when the process is completed, the disciple will be like his or her teacher"? (Luke 6:40). I hear further testimonies of their impact regularly.

I was Cheri's and Lee's pastor for nearly ten years from 1970 to 1980 (when I was still preaching *youth revivals!*). I shepherded and discipled them as new babes in Christ and saw them emerge through the disciple-making process to become rock-solid believers who were faithful in attendance, in their spiritual walk with Christ, in witnessing and soul winning, and in aspiring to make disciples. She is also the finest female soul winner I have ever known. Cheri has only in the last decade become fully aware of all the dimensions and disciplines of making disciples, and she has hit the ground running.

Cheri Holcomb is realistic enough and humble enough to know that Jesus Christ is the Actor, and that her life is only the Stage for His Performance. She echoes Paul in two life's motto verses: "To me to live is Christ" (Philippians 1:21) and "I am crucified with Christ; nevertheless

I live, yet not I, but Christ lives in me, and the life I now live in the flesh I live by the faith of the Son of God, who loved me, and gave Himself for me" (Galatians 2:20). Her greatest desire is that you would look past any human performer mentioned in this book to see Him, then capture the strategy that He modeled in His ministry and mandated in His Great Commission, and ask God to maximize this strategy in and through you—for the glory of God and the good of limitless numbers of people.

—Herb Hodges, Spiritual Life Ministries

Contents

Introduction

I would not be where I am today as a believer or as a disciple of Jesus Christ were it not for the godly men and women who have helped to shape my faith and my walk with the Lord Jesus. These have undergirded me as I have grown as a child of God. Many faithful Christians have made their personal investment in my Christian life and I have come to understand that these deposits, these vital spiritual investments, have a divine purpose. That divine purpose is to equip me to be a life-long learner and follower of Jesus Christ. Even more importantly, it is to make me a reproducer of the very same kind. I have a lofty goal for my life! I am on a course to reach the world for Christ! Though this is a lofty goal, with Christ living in me, I believe I can do just that. Following Christ's own strategy, which was modeled for me, I can leave a legacy that will count for His Kingdom's work.

The late Henrietta Mears was influential in the establishment of some of the greatest Christian outreach ministries on earth; organizations such as Campus Crusade for Christ and the Fellowship of Christian Athletes. She was also the founder of Gospel Light Publications and Forest Home Christian Conference Center. Her impact will extend far beyond her lifetime. She once said, "There is no magic in small plans. When I consider my ministry, I think of the whole world. Anything less than that would not be worthy of Christ or His will for my life."

I want to live and strive for that same kind of legacy. Christ's strategy was simple and I like simple. I need simple. Christ used ordinary people to do extraordinary things! Praise God that qualifies me! Paul wrote to Timothy in 1 Timothy 6:20, "O Timothy, guard what has been *entrusted* to you, avoiding worldly and empty chatter and the opposing arguments of what is falsely called 'knowledge'" (NASB). In 2 Timothy 1:14 he says "Guard, through the Holy Spirit who dwells in us, the treasure which has been *entrusted* to you" (NASB). I want to be found faithful with that treasure.

God has called me to make these life transference investments into other women to assist them to their highest potential in Christ. I believe it is only through the biblical principles of disciple making that this can be accomplished. Therefore, evangelizing and building other women for world impact is the strategy and the goal. I hope to make the spiritual investments necessary to leave a legacy that has further reaching returns for eternity than I will ever see in my own lifetime.

My prayer is that God will use this book as a teaching tool, as well as a challenging devotional in the lives of women, to help propel them into the greatest adventure of their own Christian lives: The Great Commission lifestyle of disciple making.

CHAPTER ONE

"Wow!" Moments and Red Tulips

My love affair with Jesus

As the deer pants for streams of water, so my soul
pants for you, O God. —Psalm 42:1

Imagine with me, the children of Israel waiting for the Word of the
Lord to be spoken. Imagine as they stood watching and waiting for their
appointed high priest to enter into the very Holy of Holies to offer sacrifice there on the alter of the mercy seat. The line of people grows; waiting for their portion, waiting for God's Word to be spoken to them. That
line would consist of the appointed high priest, then perhaps the lesser
of the priests, then the leaders of the tribes, then the men, and lastly, the
women and children, all waiting to hear from their great God.

Now let me tell you, dear one, what Jesus Christ has done for you and
for me. Because of Calvary's cross, because of that precious blood that
Jesus shed there for you and for me, we no longer have to wait at the
back of that line. When I began to discover at least some of the dimensions of this massive truth, this was indeed a "Wow!" moment for me!
Imagine now with me. I would make my way through that crowded
line, exclaiming, "excuse me please, excuse me sir, excuse me. I must

get through. I must enter into the Holy of Holies for myself, to see my Abba, my Daddy, my Father, who has a word just for me!"

Oh, beloved, what a God we serve! Are you thirsty? Do you long to know your Savior? He longs to know you intimately. Our Father waits for us to enter into the Holy of Holies to have sweet fellowship with Him. He wants to amaze us with Himself. He wants to show Himself mighty in our lives. "Call to Me and I will answer you and show you great and mighty things, fenced in and hidden, which you do not know (do not distinguish and recognize, have knowledge of and understand)" (Jeremiah 33:3 Amplified Bible). Wow! Does God ever do great and mighty things? Yes, indeed He does!

I wonder, do I truly thirst for God? What does that really mean? In a wonderful old book entitled *Titles and Symbols of Christ*, James Large writes:

> You must be aware that the Scriptures contain very frequent allusions to Rivers and Fountains, as emblematical of Christ and the blessings of salvation. And very likely the inhabitants of eastern countries understand better than we do the force of such comparisons. A recent traveler in Egypt describes the intense enjoyment with which they drink it there. "No idea can be formed in this climate of the luxury of drinking in Egypt. Little appetite for food is felt. But when, after crossing the burning sands, you reach the woods on the borders of the Nile, and pluck the fresh limes and mix their juice with the soft river water, you feel that there is no refreshment so delicious, and that no boon can be compared to water."
>
> And then it is not to Water in a cistern which can be emptied out, that Christ is compared, but to a Fountain which cannot be exhausted. Nor to Water in a lake or reservoir ever so large, which might be muddy and stagnant, but to "Living water," pure spring

Water, always fresh and flowing and sparkling with life, cool in the heat of the summer noon and clear in the storms of winter.

Beloved, what an invitation we have been given! We can come boldly—without fear of condemnation—and freely drink of this *Living Water*! Jesus is that living water. I have drunk of Him and found Him to be my total satisfaction! "I cried unto thee, O Lord: I said, Thou art my refuge and my portion in the land of the living" (Psalm 142:5 KJV). I can come boldly into His presence to "receive mercy and find my help in the time of need" (Hebrews 4:16). Imagine, no more need for a high priest to intercede for us! "For there is one God, and one mediator between God and men, the man Christ Jesus; Who gave Himself a ransom for all, to be testified in due time" (1 Timothy 2:5-6 KJV).

You will remember Elijah and one of his Wow! moments. In 1 Kings Chapter 17 we find this incredible moment of "God's bigness" showing up in Elijah's life.

Then the word of the LORD came to Elijah: "Leave here, turn eastward and hide in the Kerith Ravine, east of the Jordan. You will drink from the brook, and I have ordered the ravens to feed you there." So he did what the LORD had told him. He went to the Kerith Ravine, east of the Jordan, and stayed there. The ravens brought him bread and meat in the morning and bread and meat in the evening, and he drank from the brook. (1 Kings 17:2-6)

Now you need to understand this incredible truth—our God is not like any other god! Our God is Kadosh, "the Holy One." Our God is all-powerful and works His mighty deeds among us and so many times we miss the bigness of it all. Did you know that ravens are the only species of birds (out of thousands of species mind you), who do not feed their own young? Did you get the bigness of that, beloved? God uses a bird who does not even feed its own, to feed one of His own. Now that truly is a Wow! moment. God wants to amaze us with Himself. Have you ever had a "raven" experience with God? I have had many such Wow! moments with God. God always shows up in big ways.

One Wow! moment in particular that comes to mind is what I call my "tulip" moment. Several years ago, I had some surgery to repair two ruptured discs in my neck. This was a difficult time in my life. My friends will attest to the fact that "I don't do sick very well." The pain was tremendous in itself, but even more difficult was the long recovery after the surgery. I was introduced for the first time to the fact that believers are not exempt from depression. After the surgery I found myself battling depression for weeks and crying out to Father to heal my broken spirit.

I am so blessed to have so many wonderful close friends. Godly women in one's life are a treasure that should not be underestimated or unappreciated. During my recovery period, so many of those precious sisters in Christ came to my rescue. They came and cleaned my home and brought meals and ministered to me and to my husband in ways that we will never forget. Father used these godly servants to bring healing into my life.

If you have had a difficult surgery, you know what I mean when I say I was having one of those low days. Not only was I in pain physically, but I was just emotionally drained as well. I had awakened very early as I usually do and was walking around my house talking to Father and pouring out my complaints. Now, lest you get spiritual on me, let me remind you that our Father can handle our complaints. Psalm 77:3 says, "I remembered God, and was troubled: I *complained*, and my spirit was overwhelmed." Remember, I was low. I was weak. Our Father can handle our weaknesses! He loves to meet us just there, at the very lowest of our low. When we are at our weakest our Father comes to our rescue.

God came to *my* rescue!

The sun had not yet come up and I walked out to the front porch with a cup of coffee and stood there worshipping and telling Jesus how much I loved Him, and how thankful I was that I belonged to Him. Father understood my heart and He knew about my pain. I stood just at the edge of the porch overlooking one of my many flower gardens. This one was just beginning to spring forth with the green tips from the tulip bulbs I had planted there back in the fall. I whispered, "Oh, Father, I wish my red tulips were in bloom; you know how I love red tulips. If I just had a vase of fresh red tulips for the kitchen table, I just know that it would make me feel so much better."

I am a woman who is highly influenced by my surroundings. I am, by nature, a creature of habit as well as one whose mood is so determined by my surroundings. I love pretty things. I love God's glorious creation. I love the beauty of it all! I just knew that some red tulips would do the trick. Some flowers in the center of that kitchen table would lift my spirit and serve as an anti-depressant for my moment of despair. Ha! Do you know, beloved, that our Father knows our hearts? He loves us so much and He longs to be intimate with us. Jesus is crazy about me! I knew I could share my heart, as low as it was, with the lover of my soul. I must confess I had that all too familiar moment of "human reasoning" as well. My all too familiar flesh sprang up for a moment and I thought, "I could drop the hint to Lee as he leaves for work this morning." But I stopped and thought, "No; I'll just trust Jesus, and wait upon Him to fill that place with Himself." I just poured out my heart to my Abba.

Later that morning Heather, a dear friend of mine, called to say that she would be coming by in the afternoon for a visit and would be bringing our dinner. She said she would arrive around 1:00 that afternoon. I was excited about my friend coming to see me because I knew a visit with a sister in Christ would cheer me up. You do know that Christian friends are Jesus with skin on? I needed some tangible Jesus that day! I was sitting in the porch swing when Heather's vehicle pulled in the drive at 1:00. When she got out of her van, she turned and opened the back door to get what I assumed was dinner. When she turned around I could not believe my eyes. I was just overwhelmed. My heart was so full when I saw what she was holding in her hands. She was holding a great big vase of beautiful *red* tulips! I just burst into tears!

Heather asked, "Why are you crying?" I told her that I had been talking to Father at about 5:00 A.M. that morning, and I told her what we had been talking about. She then began to tear up and exclaimed… "You will not believe this, Cheri! At 6:00 A.M. this morning, as I stood on my back porch to pray, I was overlooking my tulip garden, which was now in full bloom. I sensed God speaking to my heart to cut you some red tulips. Knowing red tulips are my personal favorites, I set out to cut you a vase of mixed tulips." Then my friend said the most amazing thing of all. "God said to me, 'Oh no Heather, they must be all red!'" That dear sister in Christ was obedient and cut me *all* of her red tulips. Both of us began to cry and bowed our heads and prayed together. We thanked God for His amazing love for us and His incredible provision for our need. He cares both for our physical and our most intimate emotional need. He is the lover of our souls.

This kind of visitation from God is not uncommon in my life, and for this I am truly thankful. My faith journey has been a wonderful and exciting experience. It has been a consistent unfolding of Wow! moments, "tulip" moments. Isn't that what the Christian life should be? I am not saying that my life has been easy or without trial and tragedy. With Jesus Christ at the very center of my life I can say, His grace is indeed sufficient for me. His love is amazing and all consuming. The Christian life is a life of ongoing discoveries of the treasures that are ours as children of God. I hope I never get over the Wow! and the wonder of it all.

I pray that you will find this intimate relationship with Jesus to be your daily experience as you enter into the Holy of Holies each day! Father invites you to come. The Wow! moments are available. Father wants to send you some tulips!

CHAPTER TWO

The Mary Principle… Working On My A.U.G. Degree

As Jesus and his disciples were on their way, he
came to a village where a woman named Martha
opened her home to him. She had a sister called
Mary, who sat at the Lord's feet listening to what
he said.   —Luke 10:38-39

From the first day Lee and I were saved, we had Christians in our lives
that simply propelled us into the new life. It was just that, a brand new
life. These wonderful, on-fire Christians absolutely "infected us" with
the very life of Jesus. Their love and commitment to Christ preceded
everything else and this was certainly a new way of life for me. That is
what being saved means. "Therefore if any man be in Christ, he is a new
creature: old things are passed away; behold all things are become new"
(2 Corinthians 5:17 KJV). Everything became new to me. The sky was
bluer, the grass was greener, the air smelled sweeter. I was born from
above. My spirit had indeed been brought to life. I had come from a life
of drugs, alcohol and self-centered living. Of course the self-centered
lifestyle describes the lifestyle of every lost individual on earth. None

of us seek after a Holy God. We all like sheep have gone astray (Isaiah 53:6). We are all seeking our own way (Philippians 2:21).

But after I was born again, everything changed. I saw everything differently. I was so eager to learn and to grow! We were immediately involved in church; three and four times a week. We attended weekly Bible studies and went to any conference available on this pursuit of knowing the God who had moved in and changed everything. Our pastor, Brother Herb Hodges, was a wonderful shepherd who understood and was committed to building people for the Kingdom's work. We were not made to feel that we had to attend church, we wanted to be there. It was exciting to hear God's Word taught and preached and to see the result in and through the lives of God's people. We were excited to be involved in reaching our world for Christ.

I learned early the importance of hiding God's Word in my heart and was trained by it: "Thy Word have I hid in mine heart, that I might not sin against thee" (Psalm 119:11 KJV). It was not at all uncommon for Brother Herb to call on one of us in any given Sunday service to stand and recite our weekly memory passage. I was eager to do so, and you can bet I learned very early to commit myself to the daily disciplines that it took to have God's Word in my heart! I know beyond a shadow of a doubt, that this is the essential ingredient for consistency in the faith journey as well as the secret to a powerful influence for Christ in the lives of others.

A life truly transformed for the glory of God must be transformed by His Word. "Do not conform any longer to the pattern of this world, but be transformed by the renewing of your mind. Then you will be able to test and approve what God's will is—His good, pleasing and perfect will" (Romans 12:2). Our minds must be transformed by the living, active Word of God. "For the Word of God is living and active.

Sharper than any double-edged sword, it penetrates even to dividing soul and spirit, joints and marrow; it judges the thoughts and attitudes of the heart" (Hebrews 4:12). The Word of God must become the daily source for strength and power for the believer. I learned very early in my Christian walk that this was the model and the strategy for being built, as well as building others into maturing, spirit-filled believers. This is always the very basic training done with any woman God sends to me to spiritually build through the disciple-making process.

Intimacy with Christ Jesus is the heartbeat of faith and Christianity. Christianity is neither a religion nor simply a relationship. Christianity is a love affair with the Son of God. It is an intimate relationship with the Lord Jesus Christ. I heard about an anointed preacher who was once asked by an admirer, "Where did you attend school?" The preacher answered, "I went to Mary's College." "Mary's College?" the enquirer asked. "Where is Mary's College?" "It is in the thirty-ninth verse of Luke chapter ten," the preacher replied, "which says that 'Mary sat at the feet of Jesus, and heard His Word.'" The best theology degree in the world is gained in "Mary's College!"

Lee and I were married when he was seventeen and I was only fifteen. I never finished my formal education, but praise God, when I was born again I unknowingly was enrolled in "Christ's School of Life-long Learning" and I have never looked back! I do want to have a Mary's heart and I do want to earn my degree in knee-ology. I've often said that the only degree I have is my A.U.G. degree. The one I am referring to is found in the second chapter of 2 Timothy verse fifteen which says, "Study to show thyself **A**pproved **U**nto **G**od, a workman that needeth not to be ashamed, rightly dividing the word of truth" (KJV). God's Word is His incredible love letter to us and what a divine romance this truly is. As we look into the Scripture, it is important to remember that "man does not live by bread alone but by every word that proceeds out of the mouth of God" (Matthew 4:4, Deuteronomy 8:3 NASB). "All Scripture is God-breathed and is useful for teaching, rebuking, correcting and training in righteousness" (2 Timothy 3:16).

As I have grown in my personal relationship with the Lord Jesus, I have come to understand that His intent for me is to personally internalize His Word first, so that seed can first get down into my very being and change me, then it can spring upward to grow me and ultimately that Word can, and will, spring outward for the benefit of others. I must let God's Word read me, not just read God's Word I need to put myself in the story and then I am to flesh it out in the way that I live.

When we hear the Word of God taught or preached, it is always God's intent that we be changed. "And we, who with unveiled faces all reflect the Lord's glory, are being transformed into his likeness with ever-increasing glory, which comes from the Lord, who is the Spirit" (2 Corinthians 3:18). We were created for His glory, for His purpose and for His good pleasure. Colossians 1:16-18 says it perfectly:

> For by him all things were created: things in heaven and on earth, visible and invisible, whether thrones or powers or rulers or authorities; all things were created by him and for him. He is before all things, and in him all things hold together. And he is the head of the body, the church; he is the beginning and the firstborn from among the dead, so that in everything he might have the supremacy

He has created us with purpose. Ephesians 2:10 says, "For we are God's workmanship, created in Christ Jesus to do good works, which God prepared in advance for us to do." There is also a beautiful phrase hidden in the framework of Romans 1:20 which says, "For the invisible things of him from the creation of the world are clearly seen, being understood by the things that are made, even his eternal power and Godhead; so that they are without excuse" (KJV). The created world is referred to as a "work of art" or a "masterpiece." The Greek word translated "the things that are made" is the word *poiema*, the word from which we get our English word "poem." The universe is full of rhythm, rhyme and reason—it is a divine work of art. It is a masterpiece of God! And God has bequeathed this universe to His child! The word "workmanship" in Ephesians 2:10 is also a translation of the word *poema*, which means a work of art, and which is translated in one language as a "featured attraction." We are God's featured attraction, through whom He wants to attract others to Himself.

As we grow and live the Christian life, it is His divine power at work in and through us, working to flesh out or to incarnate again the very life of Jesus in and through us, so that all who see, may be drawn to Him. This is His glory being exposed or revealed in us. "To them God has chosen to make known among the Gentiles the glorious riches of this mystery, which is Christ in you, the hope of glory" (Colossians 1:27). This glory is the "outshining" of God through man. Christ lived, died and rose again, then ascended so that He could return and indwell every believer, through the Person and Presence of the Holy Spirit. You and I are to be so indwelt, so saturated with Jesus Christ that He emerges and is revealed through us. This will only be possible as we draw close to Him in that daily intimacy. This is a change that takes place inside a person through the transforming power of the Word of God and then will express itself outwardly in how we live and love others. God desires that the world see Christ in us, beloved, and therefore be drawn to Christ because of us. The Christian life is this: *It is Christ received by me, Christ resident in me, Christ reigning over me, Christ released through me and Christ ultimately realized in others because of me!*

I love the story of Mary of Bethany. This is Mary who is the sister of Martha and Lazarus. In this story we find an incredible truth about the personal impact of the Savior on Mary's life in particular. From this beautiful story we can clearly see the lasting effects that Jesus had on Mary and the lasting effects he desires to have on us and our lives and influence. This story caused me to see my relationship to Jesus and to this world in regards to "walking, talking and smelling more like Jesus" as I walk out my faith in this world. I want to leave a sweet aroma of Christ as well as a legacy that counts. I want to be remembered!

In Matthew 26:6-13 (NASB) we read:

Now when Jesus was in Bethany, at the home of Simon the leper, a woman came to Him with an alabaster vial of very costly perfume, and she poured it on His head as He reclined at the table. But the disciples were indignant when they saw this, and said, "Why this waste? For this perfume might have been sold for a high price and the money given to the poor." But Jesus, aware of this, said to them, "Why do you bother the woman? For she has done a good deed to Me. For you always have the poor with you; but you do not always have Me. For when she poured this perfume on My body, she did it to prepare Me for burial. Truly I say to you, wherever this gospel is preached in the whole world, what this woman has done will also be spoken of in memory of her."

We find this same account in Mark 14:3-8 and John 12:4-5 with a couple of pertinent things added. Mark 14:3-8 says

But some were indignantly remarking to one another, "Why has this perfume been wasted? For this perfume might have been sold for over three hundred denarii, and the money given to the poor." And they were scolding her. But Jesus said, "Let her alone;

why do you bother her? She has done a good deed to Me. For you always have the poor with you, and whenever you wish you can do good to them; but you do not always have Me. She has done what she could; she has anointed My body beforehand for the burial." (NASB)

And we see in John 12:4-5, "But Judas Iscariot, one of His disciples, who was intending to betray Him, said, 'Why was this perfume not sold for three hundred denarii and given to poor people?'" (NASB).

At the end of the passage I find the most peculiar phrase. Jesus said, "I tell you the truth, wherever this gospel is preached throughout the world, what she has done will also be told, in memory of her." Doesn't that make you curious? What had Mary done that made her to be remembered? I can tell you one thing that made Mary memorable. Her kind of worship was, and is, very costly! Women in that culture were not appreciated and certainly not of much value. So, for Mary to enter that room that day filled with men surely would have been costly. It certainly was as we see in the Scripture. The Bible says, "They became indignant of her." But her love for Jesus was more powerful than their criticism and anger, even greater than her fear. "For God hath not given us the spirit of fear; but of power, and of love, and of a sound mind" (2 Timothy 1:7 KJV). When we become intimate with the Lord Jesus, it will cost us in many ways. Many times I've had to count the cost of some friendships. Relationships in the Kingdom of God are not exempt from trial and cost any more than relationships in the world. Even the Apostle Paul had friends who later proved to be enemies of the cross and of his. Paul said, "Alexander the coppersmith did me much harm." (2 Timothy 4:14). Some can turn from friendship to hostility and enmity because of your stand for Christ.

The perfume that Mary poured on Jesus was extremely expensive in that day. In verse seven and again in verse nine it says that the perfume was "very costly and could have been sold for a high price." The story does not tell us where Mary got the perfume, but we will speculate a bit for the sake of a spiritual lesson. Perhaps this perfume was left over from Lazarus's burial? We do not know, but we do know someone had paid a great price for that perfume. So the first thing we can see is that the perfume was **bought**. That beautiful alabaster box of very costly perfume cost someone a very high price. Oh, the price that God did pay for us sinners! "For God so loved the world that He gave His only begotten Son…" (John 3:16). Revelation 5:9 says, "And they sang a new song, saying, 'Worthy are You to take the book and to break its seals; for You were slain, and purchased for God with Your blood men from every tribe and tongue and people and nation'" (NASB). God paid an incredible price for you and for me. Jesus went to the cross so that we might go free. "He made Him who knew no sin to be sin on our behalf, so that we might become the righteousness of God in Him" (2 Corinthians 5:21 NASB).

The gospel of Christ is the greatest treasure of all! It is to be valued above all else, lovingly lavished upon the lost and wastefully poured upon all those who will heed the call to come to Jesus for salvation. The gospel is that pearl of great price. This gospel you and I have been entrusted with is very precious and very, very costly. What will you do with this treasure? Mary took that costly perfume that day and she lavished it upon her Lord. That costly perfume was not only bought, but Mary **brought** it to Jesus. Mary was showing the ultimate gratitude for what Jesus had done for her. Christ had not died yet! So what had Jesus done for Mary? He had indeed given Mary an incredible gift. He raised Lazarus, her brother, from the dead. What a gift! What a promise for her own eternal life. Mary brought it to Jesus and lavished it upon Her Lord.

We live in a culture of "all about me" Christianity. We receive the gift of salvation and then we just keep it to ourselves. We have become very implosive in our Christianity rather than explosive like the Christianity modeled in the book of Acts. In Luke 14:23 we see God's strategy for reaching the lost: "Then the master told his servant, 'Go out to the roads and country lanes and make them come in, so that my house will be full.'" In our church culture today it seems we have taken on the motto: "If we build it they will come." The Christian is to be an out-going, Christ-centered person always bringing Christ to the lost. We sure do not do much bringing it to...! So many Christians think that going to church, reading their Bibles and attending Bible studies will make them a better Christian. But I am afraid Father is not much impressed by our "all about me" Christianity. We are to bring our lives and offer them on the altar as a living sacrifice.

Therefore I urge you, brethren, by the mercies of God, to present your bodies a living and holy sacrifice, acceptable to God, which is your spiritual service of worship. And do not be conformed to this world, but be transformed by the renewing of your mind, so that you may prove what the will of God is, that which is good and acceptable and perfect. (Romans 12:1-2 NASB)

Mary not only *bought* it, and then *brought* it to Jesus, but she **broke** it. Now here is her ultimate sacrifice. She did not measure it out. She just broke the alabaster box and poured it all on her Savior. Mary did not say, "Okay, here's a portion of the perfume." No, she lavished her Lord with all she had. She did not measure out her Christianity like many Christians today. Many believe that their church attendance and their Bible study attendance measure out their maturity and their faithfulness to Christ. But our church attendance is never a true measure of our love and personal devotion to Christ as Lord. Our fruits are our evidence. Jesus said in John 15:8, "My Father is glorified by this, that you bear much fruit, and so prove to be My disciples" (NASB).

Did Mary start at His head? Did she pour the perfume only on His feet? I believe Mary started at His head and let it pour all down her Lord Jesus into His beard and all over His body. Mary gave all she had and her focus was total Lordship. The Scripture says that many of those who were there watching were angered by what she did. Matthew 26:8 says, "The disciples were indignant." This kind of ministry will most often be criticized, even by the church. In John's account in John 12:4-5, "But one of His disciples, Judas Iscariot, who was later to betray Him, objected, 'Why wasn't this perfume sold and the money given to the poor? It was worth a year's wages.'" Judas was only concerned about the money. I find it very interesting that the name *Judas* means "son of perdition" and the word "perdition" is the Greek word for waste. What a waste Judas was! But Jesus said, "leave her alone"! Praise God, Jesus always comes to our rescue when we are fixed and fastened and abiding in him. I have often said that when our lives become truly saturated with Jesus Christ and we begin to truly discern His voice in our lives and follow after Him we will, excuse the phrase, hair lip the church right along with the world. We will become an offense to many and sadly even to our own brothers and sisters in Christ. Some of those we once called friends will become even as those disciples, indignant about our passion for Christ and our personal devotion to Him.

Jesus said Mary would be remembered for what she had done. But what had Mary done according to Jesus? Obviously from His perspective, Mary had done much more, had accomplished something far greater than the naked eye could see or the natural mind could comprehend. Jesus said, "She has prepared my body for burial." What? Mary did not understand that this is what she was doing. I doubt any of them did. But Mary had done something that Jesus considers most important in the believer's life. She had become intimately acquainted with Christ's death. Mary had to die to self that day. She had to put personal embarrassment aside. She had to put personal sacrifice to practice. Mary became saturated with Jesus and nothing else mattered. She had lavished her love on Christ at all costs.

The Bible says "she wiped His feet with her hair." Why did Mary wipe His feet with her hair? Oh beloved, this is huge! Because of Mary's personal sacrifice for Christ and because of her personal identification with Him that day, Mary would carry around with her, in her and on her the very "aroma of Christ" wherever she went. You just cannot hide the smell of perfume in your hair. Mary had fellowshipped in His death, perhaps even as the Apostle Paul said, "that I may know Him and the power of His resurrection and the fellowship of His sufferings, being conformed to His death" (Philippians 3:10 NASB). When Jesus went to the cross just hours later, He had that perfume on Him. That same aroma that was on Christ was on Mary as she stood there watching them crucify her Lord. There she stood and I'm sure she herself was reminded and overwhelmed by the aroma in her hair. She surely was intimately reminded of the great cost and the great sacrifice made for her that day. Mary had the aroma of that perfume on her and Jesus still had that aroma on Him, now mixed with the blood and with the sweat and the pain of death.

As she stood there at the cross and watched as Jesus laid down his life for her, she participated in His redemption. That fragrance would remind her that she was intimately acquainted with His death and intimately acquainted with His life. That fragrance began to permeate the air around her. Listen to me beloved, when you have indeed been with

Jesus in that kind of worship and intimacy you cannot hide the fact that you have been with Him, and it will be evident to others. The blessed aroma of Christ will saturate you! And all of those who stood there that day recognized that Mary had been with Jesus.

But thanks be to God, who always leads us in triumphal procession in Christ and through us spreads everywhere the fragrance of the knowledge of Him. For we are to God the aroma of Christ among those who are being saved and those who are perishing. To the one we are the smell of death; to the other, the fragrance of life. (2 Corinthians 2:14-16 NIV)

Oh that we would walk, talk and smell like Jesus! This is my heart's cry. Our lives should be that sweet aroma of Christ that will draw people to Him. All too often our Christianity is more of a repellent (a stinky Christianity), which drives people further away from Christ. Because of our lack of love and compassion and our lack of burden for the lost, many opportunities are lost for leading someone to faith in Christ. "For we are to God that aroma of Christ among those who are being saved and also to those who are perishing."

Jesus said "Wherever this gospel is preached people will be reminded of what Mary did." What was the key to Mary being remembered? Mary was personally identified with Jesus through a devoted intimacy that day. She was involved in personal sacrifice that day. This is the sacrifice that Christ has called us to. We are to take up our cross. Do you smell like Jesus? How is your personal intimacy with the Savior? Your private prayer life, your intimacy with God will always precede the power of God on your public life. Others know when we have and when we have not been with Jesus. In other words, when there is "no private intimacy, there will be no public power." I have no formal education, only my

A.U.G. degree. I want to be remembered for leaving my mark for Jesus. I want to leave a legacy that will count for His kingdoms work. Beloved, our great God is not interested in credentials. He is interested in character and only time with Him can shape us into the people of God he intends us to be. A people with spiritual clout for Jesus! "Now as they observed the confidence of Peter and John and understood that they were uneducated and untrained men, they were amazed, and began to recognize them as having been with Jesus" (Acts 4:13 NASB).

Without a daily intimate time with the Lord Jesus, we will never be remembered as Mary was. And if we are to leave a legacy that counts we must leave behind the fragrance of Christ in every place that others will be drawn to Christ as a result of our intimacy with Him.

May we yield ourselves to God so that He might fill us with the sweet Holy Spirit and cause us to walk, talk and smell like Jesus wherever we go, so that the lost will be drawn to Him. Abba, make our lives smell sweet for you! I ask this in the precious and holy name of Jesus because you said that I could! Amen.

CHAPTER THREE

Signing Up For the Course

> In the morning, O Lord, you hear my voice;
> in the morning I lay my requests before you
> and wait in expectation.   —Psalms 5:3

How do we get to that place of intimacy with Jesus? The intimate relationship with Jesus that we long for is only found when we pursue it with a vengeance! It does not just happen along. This kind of relationship must be cultivated and it takes a firm commitment and a constant dying to self. But the residuals always far outweigh any sacrifice made, and I can personally attest to this. You will have to constantly guard your daily time with the Lord. I can share with you multitudes of testimonies from disciples who have admitted at the onset of the disciple-making process that they have never had—or at least never been faithful to—a daily time with the Lord. Recently, I sat in a restaurant with several faithful disciples, fellowshipping and talking about the need and the longing for God's power on our lives. One of these precious ladies, who had recently been enlisted by one of my own disciples into the disciple-making process, said this: "Now that I'm being discipled, I realize that there is so much that I've missed. I've been a Christian for many, many years and I had never had a quiet time, nor had I ever been taught that I was supposed to have a quiet time or that it is even possible to have this kind of relationship with God." She went on to say: "The first morning I got up and started my day with a quiet time, it was absolutely invigorating and that was the first day of the rest of my life." Let me repeat what this precious saint of God said: "It was absolutely *invigorating*—and the first day of the rest of my life." The very first time she met with God He turned on the lights in her heart. Oh, beloved, our time with God is a gift, not a chore. The benefits will far exceed any sacrifice you make to have this "divine romance" that He intends for you. If you want this kind of intimacy with the Lord, you must count the cost, make the commitment and have a set strategy to follow.

Most large cities feature a zoo and many have an animal called the gnu. Usually you will find an informational plaque at each cage and on the gnu's plaque this is what they have posted. "When the gnu is under attack, it falls to its knees and fights from it knees." I just love that! "The gnu fights from its *knees*." Wow, I just wish we Christians were as wise as the gnu! When will we ever understand that we will never win any more battles than we can win from our knees? We will never have any real spiritual impact or spiritual clout for Jesus without sufficient time on our knees. The truth is we need more *knee-ology* than we do *theology* in the fellowship of believers today. There are some things that you and I can replace, and there are other things we simply cannot replace—especially when it comes to our spiritual impact for Christ. There are some things that are absolutely necessary while other things are only relatively important. The believer's daily quiet time is that *one thing* that is so vital to our spiritual growth and certainly to our impact for Christ. Some like to call it "the believer's morning watch." Others refer to it as "the daily time in the Captain's briefing room." Whatever you want to call it, our impact and our success as a Christian will come and go with our commitment to a daily quiet time. You can count on it.

Think about a deep-sea diver who is about to plunge down into the depths of a very threatening environment. He would never think of going down into the water without making sure that his air hose was connected to the tank up above. That is his source of life! What that air hose is to the deep-sea diver, the daily quiet time is to you and me as believers. It is a dangerous thing to set out for the day into our jobs or other activities or especially the temptations of that day, without first making certain that our connection with Father is intact and solid. Beloved, power checks are important.

One of the most common questions asked is "how do I have a quiet time" or, "what am I to expect from my quiet time with God"? I have learned that there are some crucial and very helpful dimensions to the daily quiet time. Here are some steps that will help to cultivate a daily practice of meeting with God that will result in a deepened romance with your Savior.

First, you need to understand the ***priority*** of your time with God. You and I always have time for the things that we love to do. Those things that are important to us are easy to get done. It is never really a question of time. It is always a question of values. The quiet time really is the barometer of the Christian life. Once you have cultivated a daily time with God, it will not take you very long to realize what you have missed when you head off into your day without it.

I learned this from personal experience many years ago. I set out one morning without adequate time with God and a witness to a lost neighbor went terribly south. This lost man told me pretty much "where I could go" and I left there just devastated. But after I got alone with Father and asked the Holy Spirit to show me what I had done wrong, the Lord spoke very tenderly and clearly. He said, "Don't dare go talk to them about Me, until you are first willing to talk to Me about them." I have learned the shame of being unprepared and I pray I never do that again. I had made the investments of technique and challenge. I had been through the courses offered through my church and I had surely seen it modeled through other faithful disciples of Christ. But nothing can replace that intimate time alone with God.

A wonderful biblical pattern for the quiet time can be seen in the principle of first fruits. When Israel went in to conquer the land of Canaan, the first city they took was devoted to God in token of His ownership of the entire land. We need to follow that same principle. The biblical rule is that the first fruits of your substance, the *first part of your day* and the *first hour of each day* should belong to God. Colossians 1:15-18 says:

> He is the image of the invisible God, the firstborn over all creation. For by Him all things were created: things in heaven and on earth, visible and invisible, whether thrones or powers or rulers or authorities; all things were created by Him and for Him. He is before all things, and in Him all things hold together. And He is the head of the body, the church; He is the beginning and the firstborn from among the dead, so that in everything He might have the supremacy.

He is worthy of the beginning of my day! He is worthy all together. It is always best to find our method and pattern from the Master. In Mark 1:35-37 we find His pattern for morning prayer:

> Very early in the morning, while it was still dark, Jesus got up, left the house and went off to a solitary place, where He prayed. Simon and his companions went to look for Him, and when they found Him, they exclaimed: "Everyone is looking for you!"

I want my prayer life to resemble His, don't you? "My voice shalt Thou hear in the morning, O Lord; in the morning will I direct my prayer unto Thee, and will look up" (Psalm 5:3 KJV). It is infinitely better to pray for help early than it is to have to yell for help late! Just as the manna was to be gathered in the morning, we should gather the treasures of the spiritual life in the morning. Do we not eat every day? I eat first thing in the morning. I do not depend on the meals I ate last week or even yesterday to sustain me. No, I need strength for each new day and so do you. Just as food is strength for our physical body, His Word is strength for our spiritual body and the battles of that day. We take time to eat every day to maintain strength and good health. We have to do the same thing for our spiritual strength. Christians cannot begin the day well, go on well, or end up well, if they have failed to make the proper provision for the day and we do that through our personal quiet time with the Lord. I cherish my time with God. It really is a matter of *priority*.

Next you need to consider the ***period*** or the time you will spend with the Lord. I am often asked "how long should a person spend in their quiet time"? "How long should my quiet time take"? Here's a good rule: "Take enough time to forget time." Amen? We tend to treat prayer like a drive through line at McDonald's. We want everything fast. We are often guilty of having a microwave mentality with God. We want Him to bless us quick. We want Him to speak to us when we want and certainly with answers to our desires. But God is into marinating, my friend! He longs for intimacy; He wants fellowship and true fellowship will take some time. Time with the Father is absolutely vital. Prayer is our time to get exposed to God, not to try to get God to hurry up and get in line with us and our agenda. You and I need to be exposed to His way of thinking and that is what studying His Word does. That time of prayer and study secures and adjusts you and me to His will and His way. Too often our prayer is our list of wants and needs. We should offer our Father the blank page for each day and ask Him to fill it and bless it. Just think about this. We are invited by the very Majesty on high to come and sit and to receive His Word, His anointing, and His blessing for that day!

George Muller, the great man of faith from Bristol, England, said, "A believer's first responsibility with each new day is to bring his own soul into a happy relationship before God." Our goal should be to seek God's face each day, before we dare to see the face of any man. You are reserving the most strategic part of your day for this very purpose. This is truly your "briefing session in the Captain's Room." Everything else is useless and in vain without time before God's throne.

In a Spanish art gallery, there is a painting that shows a laborer plowing a field with a plough attached to a yoke of oxen. He has completed half the field, but he has gotten into a fresh furrow and knelt on his knees. His eyes are closed and his hands are folded in prayer. In the distant background may be seen the spire of a church, which apparently has rung out the call to prayer. But there is something the laborer does not know. As he is on his knees, an angel from heaven has descended from the skies, picked up his plough, has completed one row, and is turning the oxen to plough the next row. Under the picture there is this caption: *No Time Lost.* When you and I take time to meet with our great God, we never lose any time—we gain eternity.

Next you should consider the ***parts*** of your quiet time. What do I need with me to have a quiet time with God? There are certain materials you should use in that time alone with God. I recommend at least two good translations of the Bible. I use a New American Standard Version, New International Version, as well as the Amplified Bible. There is a wonderful tool on the internet called Biblegateway.com which I use daily as I study. You also need to have a couple of good daily devotional books. There are a lot of inspiring devotionals available. *Daily With the*

King, by Glyn Owens is an excellent devotional. Keep a journal for notations while you pray and study. Make a prayer list and keep a globe or a world map in view. *Operation World* by Patrick Johnstone is an excellent book to enlarge your vision for world impact.

Then there is a ***procedure*** you should follow. Here are some suggestions for a pattern to follow. First, get quiet enough to listen! Do you really listen? We live in a fast-paced world and this is especially true as wives and mothers. We are inundated with words all day long. This will have to be a cultivated thing in your life. You will have to work at it. We need to sit in God's presence expecting Him to speak to us. Be like King David, "who went in and sat before the Lord" in 2 Samuel 7:18. Come before your God with an expectant heart. Then pray. When you pray, pray believing God. I pray with great expectation and a wonderful anticipation for God's moving in my heart and in my life. God loves to answer our prayers when they are prayers of faith and expectancy.

Andrew Murray said about prayer:

Beware in your prayer, above everything of limiting God, not only with unbelief, but by fancying that you know what He can do. Expect unexpected things, *above all that we ask or think*. Each time you intercede, be quiet first and worship God in His glory. Think of what He can do, of how He delights to hear Christ, of your place in Christ; and expect great things. (Emphasis added.)

I also recommend that you begin your prayer like the psalmists. Psalm 119:18 "Open Thou mine eyes, that I might behold wondrous things out of Thy law" (KJV). Remind yourself of Psalm 119:130, "The unfolding of Your words gives light; it gives understanding to the simple" (NASB). We simply need to understand that unless God turns on the lights, we will miss it! Ask God to make you "simple" enough to receive

His light during the time you spend with Him. Read the Word out loud. Read His Word the way you would picture a lover reading a love-letter from his beloved. That is exactly what your Bible is! It is God's love letter to you! We need to remember that every day we have been given the invitation and the honor of sitting down with the Book that contains the very words of the One who created us, and who loved us enough to pay an infinite price to have a relationship with us. Go into the Holy of Holies each day, spread your Bible there on the Mercy Seat, and read it in the light of the bright Shekinah of God's Glory and Presence. I tell you, dear heart, He is absolutely crazy about you and waiting each day to sing over you. "The LORD your God is with you, He is mighty to save. He will take great delight in you, He will quiet you with His love, He will rejoice over you with singing" (Zephaniah 3:17).

The next dimension of your quiet time is the ***purpose*** for it. Why am I having a quiet time with God anyway? What will it truly benefit me? I love the burning bush story in Exodus chapter three. You will notice that it was not until Moses "turned aside" to see this unusual thing that God spoke and revealed Himself to Moses. Our quiet time is for that very same purpose. It is for our "turning aside" from everything and everyone else just to meet with God. This time with Father is not just for learning principles or gleaning new spiritual truths from the Word. But it is more to cultivate a personal relationship with a person. I am having a love affair with Jesus! The time I spend with Him is to cultivate a spiritual romance with Him! Elizabeth O'Connor said, "We are called first of all to belong to Jesus Christ as Savior and Lord, and to keep our lives warmed at the hearth of His life." The Word of God is not so much for our pursuit of its precepts as it is a personal encounter with the living God! The reason you and I should practice our daily quiet time is not just to get our needs met; but to turn away or look away from everything and everyone else and to look unto Jesus, the author and finisher of our faith. "Let us fix our eyes on Jesus, the author and perfecter of our faith, who for the joy set before Him endured the cross, scorning its shame, and sat down at the right hand of the throne of God" (Hebrews 12:2). "And we, who with unveiled faces all reflect the Lord's glory, are being transformed into His likeness with ever-increasing glory, which comes from the Lord, who is the Spirit" (2 Corinthians 3:18).

And then finally, there is the ***protection*** of your daily time with God that needs to be addressed. Remember the principle: what counts costs. Satan cares very little about how many Bible studies you and I have attended or taught, or how much money we give to missions or how many church services we have faithfully attended. But when you get a woman *personal with* God, you will find a woman *powerful for* God! Our enemy will take note of that and he will do everything in his power to distract you from your time with God because he knows full well what it will afford you. The enemy knows what time in God's presence and in His Word will do in, and more importantly, through your life. You will have to guard your time alone with God if you are going to keep it and have that true impact that Christ intended.

It is so important to remember that in the economy of God, *"go hide thyself"* in 1 Kings 17:3 always comes before the *"go show thyself"* in 1 Kings 18:1. Effective public ministry will only follow efficient private ministry. If we hide ourselves daily in the Presence of God, as Elijah did in obeying God, then we will do well in our encounters with the Ahabs of life. But, if not, we'll have to "sponsor ourselves"—and just take the losses! Think of what is at stake, beloved, when you do not spend that time with God. This quiet time with God is our vital prep time! It is preparing us for an eternity to come. Dr. Raymond Edman was speaking to Wheaton College students about how we should prepare to meet with

God, when suddenly he slumped onto the pulpit, fell to the floor.... and literally entered into the Presence of the King! How would you approach tomorrow morning's quiet time if you knew that you would actually die while you were in it—and actually enter face-to-face into the King's Presence?

One day you and I will meet together in our King's Presence. I think we had better make sure that we are not on unfamiliar territory or in strange company when that day comes!

Remember...when a woman becomes *personal with* God, she also becomes *powerful for* God. God always uses the vessel that lies closest at hand!

CHAPTER FOUR

A Life Shaped by a Cross

Then Jesus said to His disciples, "If anyone wishes
to come after Me, he must deny himself, and take
up his cross and follow Me."

—Matthew 16:24; Also in Luke 9:23

The Word of God is sweet; it is sweet to the ear and satisfies the long-
ings of my heart. The psalmist said in Psalm 19:9-10, "The fear of the
LORD is pure, enduring forever. The ordinances of the LORD are sure
and altogether righteous. They are more precious than gold, than much
pure gold; they are sweeter than honey, than honey from the comb." I
love encouraging words like, "be of good courage, I have overcome the
world." Or "I will never leave nor forsake you," or "Take my yoke upon
you for it is easy." But, sometimes God's Word is tough to handle. It
sometimes is like sandpaper against my flesh. Learning to "flesh out"
God's Word is vital. We must learn to take it in and then flesh it out
in the way that we live. There is a constant dying to self that must take
place on a daily basis. I know me. I know my old hard selfish heart. But,
I also know the power of the Word of God. As we take it in daily, it truly
does have a transforming power.

As I seek to be a disciple and a disciple maker, I am constantly aware
of my own need to decrease, so that Jesus might increase in my life.

John the Baptist said "He must increase, but I must decrease" (John 3:30 NASB). Apart from Him, I can do nothing! My goal as a disciple maker is to live, or to flesh it all out, so that *others* have a model before them. I want to live a life worth following for the glory of God and the fulfillment of the Great Commission. I know that in myself, in my flesh there is nothing good. But Christ living His life in and through me can accomplish even the impossible. The only way to live this kind of life, a life worth following is through a daily dying to self and allowing Christ to live his life through us. I must cooperate with the Holy Spirit on this road of sanctification. I like to think of sanctification as "God beating the Cheri out of me" so that the Jesus in me can be more clearly seen and heard. When I do not cooperate through a life of submission and surrender the ride can get pretty rough, but all for Jesus sake and for my good.

Here in the text of Matthew 16, Christ lays out His requirements for discipleship and frankly, His words are not so easy to hear. His words here are demanding and it is when we hear the demands or the requirements of discipleship that we begin to truly count the cost of following Jesus. This text is in a command form. It is a mandate for each believer. The Christian life mandates a crucified practice. These are the demands of discipleship: "If anyone wants to follow me, let him deny himself, take up his cross, and follow me." Note the connection between the two phrases about our self-denial and our cross-bearing. The denial of self is that hidden, personal and internal process, while the taking up of the cross is the outward and external manifestation of that self-denial.

Take that last part first. "Let him...take up his cross." As we mature as Christians, we discover along the way that the cross is not only the way *to* life, it is the only way *of* life. I'm not only saved by the cross, I am also saved *into* the cross and ultimately my life is shaped *by* the cross! Sinners come *to* the cross to be saved, and the saint comes *from* the cross in order to serve. Salvation lifts the load of sin from my back—but it is replaced with the load of a cross. But just what did Jesus mean when He said that taking our cross is mandatory for a disciple? What does it really mean to take up our cross?

I have come to understand that this is a ***prescribed commitment***. Our cross is something we have to accept ("take up"). The nature of our cross is not for us to decide. We do not choose it for ourselves. We are to simply take it. You do not have to go and search for it. According to Jesus, each Christian has their cross waiting for them, a cross destined and appointed by God. I believe the most misunderstood concept of the disciple's cross is the misunderstanding of what that cross truly is. It is very important that we have a clear understanding of this if we are going to have any real spiritual influence for Christ and His Kingdom's work. You see, your cross is not merely the hardships, or sorrows, or disappointments of your life. It's not a sickness or bereavement, or a misfortune. Your cross and my cross is a necessary sacrifice. Isn't that what His cross was? His cross was necessary for my redemption. This means we will have to sacrifice to be personally involved in the redemption of others. There is that "others" thing again. You and I will have to give up whatever we have to in order to truly serve Christ and be personally involved in the salvation of others. All the other things mentioned may be thorns-in-the-flesh, but they are not our cross to bear. So let me say it again so it will be clear. Yours and my cross is anything it costs us to be personally involved in seeing others come to Christ.

There are several things that happen when a Christian takes up his cross. First, there will be a *drastic renunciation of self*. Self begins to get smaller and Jesus begins to get bigger in life. There must be and will be an awareness of the ever enlarging presence and power of the Savior in your life when you die to self. Second, when a Christian takes up his cross, there will be a *definite rejection by society*. When we walk in this kind of relationship with Jesus, we will *separate* far more in society than we *gather* together. The truth is, as you study the life and ministry of Jesus, you will find that He scattered a lot more crowds than he gathered. Jesus told us that when we love Him and obey His commandments that the world wouldn't like us very much. Actually, Jesus warned us that we would be hated. When you begin to take up your cross and truly follow Jesus for the sake of other's salvation, many will reject you and even hate you. Third, when a Christian takes up a cross and follows Jesus, there is a *dynamic recognition of the Savior*. Jesus said, "But I, when I am lifted up from the earth, will draw all men to myself" (John 12:32). Finally, when a Christian truly takes up his cross and follows Jesus, there will be a *divine revelation of salvation* among sinners as well as a reward for the cross-carrying saint. A sold-out follower of Christ is a fisher of souls and a soul winner!

Not only is cross-bearing a prescribed commitment for the believer, it also involves a ***personal commitment***. I have to take it up. We are called to *take* our cross; we are not called to *make* our cross. And we need to understand that we are to take up *our* cross, not Christ's cross. You and I cannot take up His cross. He took it up alone, and then in a divine mystery, He made it possible for you and me to take up our cross and find the virtue and power of His cross; but we must take up our own cross.

Our crosses may be hewn from different trees,
But we all must have our Calvaries.

I heard about a young man who was pondering the claims of Christ. He asked an older Christian, "And what happens if I don't follow Jesus?" The veteran Christian replied, "That's just it, son. Nothing happens!

You just sink back into oblivion!" So cross-bearing is an inherent part of the Christian life, and it begins with a personal commitment. It begins in that hour when, in the depths of our will, we resolve at any and every cost to follow Jesus Christ.

But, I tell you, taking up our cross can and will be obvious to others and necessary for others. Taking up our cross also involves a ***public commitment***. I've never heard of a private crucifixion, have you? The very nature of crucifixion, as well as its purpose, demands a public act! They did not crucify men at night. They were not taken to a secluded place to be nailed to their crosses. They were nailed to their crosses openly and publicly. Beloved, crucifixion was a public act, intended to have a public impact and our cross-bearing is designed by God to have a public impact as well. There is simply no such thing as a 007 spy for Jesus! There is no undercover Christianity here! When a Christian carries his cross, the Savior will be plainly seen, and sinners will be powerfully saved.

It doesn't end here. Taking up our cross involves not only a prescribed commitment, a personal commitment and a public commitment; taking up your cross is a ***painful commitment***. There is absolutely no such thing as a painless crucifixion! There is no comfortable cross! But the cost of this life is one of its most attractive features, and one of the great tragedies is that we have offered a Christianity that comes at bargain basement prices and reduced rates. Is there any wonder why there are still so many lost people around us, when we have so many more technologies, more churches, more platforms and more opportunities for proclaiming the gospel than ever before? Beloved, there is no "Bargain Basement" cross. Christ's cross did not come cheap!

In one of his books, Dr. Earl Allen tells of an incident that occurred while he was on a trip to the Holy Land. In a village in Israel, the group of tourists was met by a native peddler with a small cart of merchandise.

The man's clothing was faded with age. His shoes were worn and shapeless; his hat was large and ragged. His beard and long hair nearly covered his face. Dr. Allen said he would have passed the man without noticing him if he had not heard what he was saying. In broken English and with a shrill voice, he was crying out, "A cross! A cross! A cheap cross! Will anyone buy a cheap cross?" In those surroundings, the man didn't seem out of place. He was simply selling little metal crosses as Holy Land souvenirs.

But in today's culture of Christianity we often hear those same words sounding softly and attractively from our Christian podiums, pulpits, and platforms. Jesus Christ does not offer a cheap cross! The cross you and I are to take up in His Name is costly and it's painful.

Taking up our cross involves not only a prescribed commitment, a personal commitment, a public commitment, and a painful commitment, taking up our cross involves a ***persistent commitment*** to be sure. Luke 9:23 adds one word to the demand: ".... let him take up his cross *daily*." Someone has described this cross-bearing life as "a spread out surrender." The truth is it would be a lot easier to take up a cross and die on it once than to take up all the little crosses day by day and die a deeper death upon each one of them. But the flesh, or the self-life, is like the proverbial cat with nine lives (except that our flesh has even more than that), and has to be daily crucified and denied. Maxie Dunham said it graphically, "Every time I try to die to self, the devil calls in his Harvey Team and they 'work like the devil' to keep the carnal man, who trusts in himself, alive." Listen; though Jesus spoke of taking up our cross, did you notice that He never spoke of laying it down? Every day we have to look "death to self" squarely in the face and choose it as our mode of life for that day. Cross-bearing involves a persistent commitment.

Then finally, taking up our cross is a ***purposeful and productive commitment***. We so easily overlook the primary purpose of the Christian's cross. *The primary purpose of a cross is to redeem other people!* And, to see others saved! Our cross is whatever it costs us to be continually involved in Christ's soul-saving mission. So, just go over that list again: Our commitment to follow Jesus is *prescribed*, it is *personal*, it is *public*, it is *painful*, and it must be *persistent*, and praise God, it is *purposeful and productive*! At this point, we need to be very careful to keep a clear distinction here between Christ's cross and ours. In no way am I suggesting that the disciple's cross is equal in its significance to the Savior's cross. Jesus bore His cross in order to *accomplish* redemption; we bear our cross in order to *announce* the redemption that He accomplished. What a Savior! What a gospel! And just as there was no salvation for us without His cross, there won't be any salvation of others without our cross. The world is looking for our cross so that they can clearly see Jesus.

Dietrich Bonhoeffer said, "To be a Christian is to suffer with God, in a godless world, for people who do not in any way deserve to be suffered for." We *must* die to self. A missionary told a story of his boyhood days on a Wisconsin farm when the family was being haunted by hunger. One day his father went down to the cellar and brought out the few potatoes that were left after that long, hard winter. He said to the family, "We have got to plant these." His wife cried out in protest, "You cannot do that; we will have nothing to eat!" But the father insisted. The mother stood weeping as she saw those few remaining potatoes being cut to pieces and buried in the garden. However, in the fall the picture had changed. There was a good harvest of potatoes—food for many months—that resulted from the earlier planting. The mother would have kept those few potatoes, rationed them to her family, and possibly starved. The father "lost" them by burying them and found them again, found them all new and multiplied.

So, Jesus laid down these claims as the first requirement of a disciple's life. He said, "Whoever will save his life (selfishly hoard it) shall lose it, and whoever will lose his life for My sake shall find it." Are you sparing your life or spending it on Christ and others? Jesus also said, "I tell you the truth, unless a kernel of wheat falls to the ground and dies, it remains only a single seed. But if it dies, it produces many seeds" (John 12:24). This kind of life is only found as we die to self.

One of my favorite stories was told by Pastor Charles Crowe. Dr. Crowe was a pastor in Chicago, Illinois. One morning as Dr. Crowe drove around the Chicago loop to his church, he saw an unusual sight. His church has atop it "the tallest steeple of any church in the world." And as he approached the church that morning, he saw a large crowd of people standing on the front sidewalk, looking upward. He parked his car and joined them, also looking up to see what they were gazing at. High up on the metal cross on top of the steeple, a painter was belted into place and painting his way down the cross. The cross could be seen conspicuously swaying in the air. After watching a while, Dr. Crowe left and went into his office and suddenly the Holy Spirit brought a spiritual lesson to his mind. That cross has been there every day, but previously, it drew no crowd on the sidewalk. Why the crowd today? The answer came: Today there was a man on that cross, and it is the combination of the cross and the man that demanded their attention.

I believe the world is unconsciously saying the same thing to us— today. It is only as we take up our cross that people will see Jesus, and only as they see Jesus, will they be transformed into His likeness (2 Corinthians 3:18). Lift up your eyes! Gird up your loins! Take up your cross! As we do, many will rise up and join us in serving Jesus. The

Apostle Thomas said, "Unless I see in His hands the imprint of the nails, and put my finger into the place of the nails, and put my hand into His side, I will not believe" (John 20:25 NASB).

This kind of life—the cross bearing life, will have a *purposeful* impact. I first saw this modeled for me in the life of a woman who poured herself into me and many other young mothers for years. Mrs. Jewel Noah, now in heaven, was one of those precious cross-bearing women, sold out to Jesus Christ and to His purpose for her and her life. I met Mrs. Noah in 1976, shortly after I was saved and an active member of Cherokee Baptist Church in Memphis, Tennessee. Brother Herb, our pastor, introduced me to Mrs. Noah and my life was off on an incredible course of disciple making. We met in Mrs. Noah's home weekly for Precept Bible study and prayer. For those few and formative years I grew quickly to understand my purpose in the Kingdom's work and my Father's appointment for my life and ministry. It was this precious saint of God who spoke courage into my life; courage to make a difference and to follow after Jesus at all costs.

Positive words of encouragement and affirmation make a tremendous impact on us and can certainly catapult us on our way upward towards maturity in our faith walk. I remember well the first time Mrs. Noah said to me, "Cheri, I believe God has marked you for greatness!" Now again, before you think me prideful, let me explain something very important. God has destined each one of us for greatness. "For I know the plans I have for you," declares the LORD, "plans to prosper you and not to harm you, plans to give you hope and a future" (Jeremiah 29:11). Our problem is understanding greatness from God's point of view. If we are honest with ourselves, we will admit to this need to please. Mrs. Noah saw something in me, and that something being Jesus, and she simply nurtured that seed for God's purposes and glory. She told me that I had a speaking gift. I didn't understand really what that meant, but to hear her say it thrilled my heart. I wanted to please Mrs. Noah and I especially wanted to be useful and to please my Lord. This sweet saint would pour her time and love into me as well as challenge me like no one else did. Mrs. Noah, along with Brother Herb made memorizing Scripture a vocation for me. It cultivated a love for the Word of God.

One of the fondest memories I have of this wonderful disciple maker was when she presented an opportunity to me that truly shaped my Christian life in regard to evangelizing. Mrs. Noah asked me one morning after Bible study to do something with her and, if I agreed to it, I was not to tell anyone about it. It would be just between the two of us. I agreed, of course, mostly out of curiosity but also because I loved Mrs. Noah. She told me where to meet her, and at what time, and not to be late. Mrs. Noah was a disciplined woman who demanded likewise from her disciples. I was instructed to meet her that following Friday morning at 7:00 A.M. at a convenience store not far from my home. When I arrived, she told me to leave my car there and to join her in her car for a drive. We drove and drove and drove. I had no idea where we were going but I did not even care. I was with Mrs. Noah and I loved and trusted that dear saint and so appreciated any time she invested in me. We drove for about forty minutes and landed at the naval base in Millington, Tennessee. She pulled into the housing facility there and parked the car and then looked over at me and said, "You just watch and pray, dear! That's all, just watch and pray!"

And so I did just that. I simply watched and prayed. And how moved I was as we went door to door; I simply watched this incredible, loving, quiet-spirited woman of God present the gospel of Jesus Christ, using a Four Spiritual Laws Tract. She shared Jesus with everyone and anyone who would listen. That first day at the naval base we had several of the navy wives pray with us to receive Christ as Lord and Savior. I tell you, I was absolutely overjoyed and I was hooked! Mrs. Noah and I made the trip to that naval base for several weeks consistently; me just watching and praying, just watching and praying. But then, one morning as we arrived there in the parking lot, Mrs. Noah looked over at me and said, "Okay darling, now I watch and pray!" And, you know what? I did not even argue. I wasn't even really afraid. I was so ready to experience the obvious joy I saw in her and had certainly had ample time to "catch" it and had the best teacher anyone could have in the simplicities of "flinging the seed" of the gospel of Christ. That precious disciple maker infected me with a passion to share the gospel with a holy boldness. "I am not ashamed of the gospel, because it is the power of God for the salvation of everyone who believes: first for the Jew, then for the Gentile" (Romans 1:16).

Mrs. Noah certainly carried her cross and many were drawn to Christ as a result of her selfless lifestyle. I remember her home going and the celebration service for her life. Her impact had such a far reaching effect on others and that day many of us who had spent that time in her home were moved at the living picture of generational disciple making. When Brother Herb spoke of her life and testimony during her eulogy, he asked if there were any women there that day who could stand as a testimony to Jewel Noah's life's investment in them and to all of our amazement, just about every woman in that place stood to their feet to give testimony to a life that truly left a spiritual legacy through a Great Commission lifestyle of disciple making.

I not only thank God for Mrs. Jewel Noah, but I want to live that kind of life. I want to fulfill that word spoken over my life. I want to leave my mark for Jesus sake. "A student is not above his teacher, but everyone who is fully trained will be like his teacher" (Luke 6:40). Mrs.

Noah was a wonderful teacher and disciple maker. Her life clearly reflects a generational legacy. She is worth more to God even today than she was while alive. The truth is, we should all be worth more to God after we are dead and gone than while alive because our legacy and ministry of multiplication should clearly go on and on and on as a result of obedience to Christ's command to reproduce through the standard of disciple making. We must get personally involved. We must be at it and always at it…until the end of this age; thus fulfilling our part in the Great Commission mandate of disciple making.

Dietrich Bonhoeffer said, "The truly righteous person lives for the next generation." Mrs. Noah lived for the next generation in making the necessary sacrifices and spiritual deposits in my life and the lives of so many other women. We will never know on this side of heaven all the lives that have been impacted and the spiritual down line left for Christ and for His Kingdom through this one simple woman who loved God and walked in obedience to His command to "turn people into disciples." I can hardly wait to see my precious spiritual mother when I arrive at my heavenly destination.

I pray that as I stand before the throne of God that many women will stand behind me as a result of a life surrendered to Jesus Christ and to His Great Commission lifestyle of disciple making. I am convinced that the kind of heaven that is before me then will depend on the kind of people who are lined up behind me now.

CHAPTER FIVE

Turn on the Lights, God

Wherefore I also, after I heard of your faith in the Lord Jesus, and love unto all the saints, Cease not to give thanks for you, making mention of you in my prayers; That the God of our Lord Jesus Christ, the Father of glory, may give unto you the spirit of wisdom and revelation in the knowledge of him: The eyes of your understanding being enlightened; that ye may know what is the hope of his calling, and what the riches of the glory of his inheritance in the saints, And what is the exceeding greatness of his power to us-ward who believe, according to the working of his mighty power, Which he wrought in Christ, when he raised him from the dead, and set him at his own right hand in the heavenly places, Far above all principality, and power, and might, and dominion, and every name that is named, not only in this world, but also in that which is to come: And hath put all things under his feet, and gave him to be the head over all things to the church, Which is his body, the fullness of him that fills all in all.   —Ephesians 1:15-23 KJV

Some of the most profound lessons I have learned are concerning that of walking in the Spirit and seeing things from God's perspective. It is vital that we understand that God has given to us every spiritual blessing we need concerning our heavenly possessions. "Praise be to the God and Father of our Lord Jesus Christ, who has blessed us in the heavenly realms with every spiritual blessing in Christ" (Ephesians 1:3 NASB). Our spiritual eyes need to be trained and they are trained by His Spirit for our seeing and appropriation of divine spiritual truth. We must understand that only God can reveal God. The human intellect alone, no matter how advanced, can never understand the mind and the heart of God. We need God to turn on the lights and reveal Himself to us. The psalmist asked of God in Psalm 119:18, "Open my eyes that I may see wonderful things in your law" (NASB). He also said in Psalm 119:130, "The unfolding of Your words gives light; it gives understanding to the simple" (NASB). It is vital that we as believers learn to be careful not to mishandle holy things. Too often, we read our Bibles as if we are checking off our spiritual duty for that day and we simply miss the magnificence of it all.

In some Bibles, the publishers have added an editorial note to each text of Scripture to help the reader discern the basic theme of the coming paragraph. In one of my Bibles just before the text there is posted in the margin "Insight," and in another "Knowledge and Understanding." They are both accurate. I believe the words in the following prayer contain the most important single prayer that any human being can pray for another human being at any time. I do not believe it is possible to pray a more important prayer for yourself or for anyone else.

In Paul's great prayer, found in Ephesians 1:15-23, there are some incredible truths that can open our eyes to some very important things. First, by way of observation, notice in Paul's prayer that he starts by revealing a *mood*. Paul is obviously in a certain kind of mood. Paul writes, "For this reason" or "wherefore." The word "wherefore" or "for this reason" in verse 15 reveals that Paul is in a very *thoughtful mood* about what he is writing. Now remember, the word 'wherefore' is a connecting word and so whenever we read a word like that in a text of Scripture, we should always ask ourselves, "What's the wherefore there for?" This is amazing because when you look back at the preceding verses or the initial thoughts and words that Paul has written already, you discover that the Apostle Paul has just written the greatest single sentence ever written. It's an incredibly long sentence. It's so long, that it probably wouldn't pass any grammatical structure test in any classroom. But remember, Paul is not at all interested in grammar; he is only interested in grace! Amen?

As far as we know, this is the longest single sentence ever recorded in literature. The sentence is twelve verses long in the biblical text, and some of the verses are lengthy by themselves. So, Paul has just written a celebration with his words of the Christians understanding of the grace of God. He has just celebrated, verbally, grace as the very source, the very reason, and the very cause and producer of our salvation. Now, that is pretty huge in itself! But, it is also obvious from the beginning of Paul's prayer that he is also in a *thrilled mood*. He says to the Ephesian Christians, "I heard of your faith in the Lord Jesus, and love for all the saints." What a testimony! What a tribute to the Ephesian Christians! There is no pastor on earth who would not be absolutely thrilled with these two things actively evident among his people, faith in the Lord Jesus, and love for all the saints.

We need to take note of the order of the two; because the order of the two is especially important in regards to the Christian experience. Paul mentions, "Faith in the Lord Jesus," then he says, "love for all the saints."

These two features have a cause-and-effect relationship in the Christian life. If the one is present, then the other will be also. But, if one is absent, they both will be absent. Only the person who is rightly related to the Lord Jesus by faith will be rightly related to others in love. It's the picture of the cross. So Paul is *thrilled* with the Ephesians and the evidence of these things actively working in their lives.

Notice that Paul is not only in a *thoughtful* and a *thrilled mood*; Paul is also in a *thankful mood*. He writes, "I do not cease to give thanks for you, making mention of you in my prayers." The Greek word translated, "I give thanks" is ("eucharisteo") and is used twenty-three times by Paul, and only fourteen times in the rest of the New Testament. What a statistic! Paul is just always giving thanks. Here is one of the gigantic secrets of Paul's incredible Christian life and his influence. While everybody else is thinking about self, and planning and praying, and living their Christian lives for themselves, Paul is always thinking and focusing on *others*. While so many lived "outside-in" lifestyles, Paul lived an "inside-out" lifestyle, always thinking about others. He was constantly praying and thanking God for someone in his life. There it is again, that others thing.

Jesus was like that with His twelve disciples. He invested in them, or really, He infected them with Himself. Then after he saturated them with Himself, He sent them away from Himself to do the very same thing with others. The mandate of disciple making is an others-focused ministry. To be others focused we must strive for unity in the body of Christ. Jesus said, "By this all men will know that you are My disciples if you have love for one another" (John 13:35 NASB). The best definition and illustration I have ever heard is of course from my Papaw. Herb said once that the best picture of unity and humility is found in the Holy Trinity. The Father is always promoting the Son; the Son is always promoting the Father; and the Holy Spirit is always promoting the Son. We never see them self-advancing. Herb said, "They are always trying to out-humble one another." I love that! "Behold, how good and how pleasant it is for brothers to dwell together in unity!" (Psalm 133:1). "Beyond all these things, put on love, which is the perfect bond of unity" (Colossians 3:14).

So, in Paul's prayer in Ephesians we see that Paul was in a *thoughtful, thrilled,* and *thankful mood.* If we then would begin by being more thoughtful, if we would get excited about the things of God and show our love and support for what God is doing in the lives of other people, we would see such a change in the church today. We should also notice that there is a sequence or a spiritual progression from verses three through fourteen and then it comes to a climax when you get to this prayer in verse fifteen. Remember again the "wherefore" of verse fifteen. What is the "wherefore" there for? Remember that Paul has been celebrating! It is almost as if Paul is straining with the language, piling words on top of words to express all that God is and all that God has done for us through Christ Jesus our Lord. The Apostle Paul prays with great joy and thankfulness for them in light of this massive truth.

Remember the two marginal titles, a prayer for "knowledge" and "understanding," or "insight"? This is an incredible prayer for spiritual illumination, a prayer for God to turn on the lights. What an incredibly important prayer it is! In verse eighteen we see the ***significance of illumination***. Why is illumination so important? Well, the effectiveness of any truth in our lives depends on our apprehension or our understanding of it. If a truth only sits there neatly arranged on the shelf, it won't move us very far, will it? It's like the Discovery Channel on television. We must turn it on and tune in. That tube must have light brought to it or no show. The Bible is the greatest "discovery channel" in the world! But just like our television set has to be turned on and tuned in—flooded with light in effect, so we too must have the Holy Spirit in us enlightening us to the undiscoverable truths that lie beneath the surface. It is not possible for the unaided human mind, regardless of its natural brilliance, to understand the mind of God in Scripture without the miracle of divine illumination.

I heard a story about a family who were entertaining another family one evening in their home, and after dinner, they had all gathered in the family room for fellowship and a visit. Their little four-year-old was sitting on the floor playing quietly with some of his toys and just when there was a slight lull in the conversation, the child blurted out, repeating something he had heard his older brother say earlier in the day as he was reciting his math assignment from school: "Two times two is four," the little boy said thoughtlessly. Suddenly, everyone gasped when they heard this from a four-year-old. The mother just knew that they had a child genius! She asked proudly, "What did you say, dear? Say it again." The little boy, surprised at the attention he was now getting, said again, "Two times two is four." And the two families expressed their amazement that a child so young could know so much. Then suddenly, while they were discussing the boy's brilliance, he interrupted again and asked, "Mommy, what's a two?" You see, he had *information without illumination*. This is exactly the problem with most Christians in regards to God's Word. They have a lot of information, but no spiritual illumination.

There are a lot of sophisticated cameras on the market today. These cameras have two shutters. One shutter covers the lens and the other covers the film. You open one to prepare to use the camera, and then you open the other to snap the picture. The one corresponds to the new birth and the other to spiritual illumination. Our new birth is only the beginning. The new birth gives us the spiritual eyes to see with, and then prepares them for use. But we need ongoing understanding of every immediate picture that God brings before us. And this ongoing understanding comes to the individual exactly the same way the new birth comes by a miracle of Almighty God produced in the heart of the person.

John Calvin said, "Illumination is like a pair of spectacles. Without it, our vision may be blurred, but with it, we can see clearly." The psalmist said, "In Thy light shall we see light." On a visit to New York City a few years ago, I was amazed at the sights of the city, but I was especially captivated with St. Patrick's Cathedral in Manhattan. When we arrived, it was just at dusk and the evening lights were beginning to illuminate the building and it was beautiful. Those stained glass windows are sixty feet tall and each one full of color and beauty. But, when we went back to the cathedral the second time during the afternoon when the sun was shining the difference was amazing. As I stood there and surveyed the details of those stained glass windows, Father opened my eyes to see them with new revelation. The absolute brilliance of those windows was incredible. The sun brought out colors and shapes and such detail that we totally missed when there was no sunlight. You see, with the absence of the sunlight we could not see all of the astounding brilliance and beauty of those stained glass windows. The light showed the splendor of all their beauty. Now, I had the power of sight before, but I had no light. What the sun is to those windows, the Holy Spirit is to the student of the Word of God. To see, we must have both sight and light. If we have sight but no light, we cannot see what's there. If we have light but no sight, we still cannot see. Both sight and light are absolutely essential for us to see spiritually. Only God can reveal God!

Paul also identifies the nature and the *source of this illumination*. In verse eighteen he uses the word "heart." The King James Bible translates it "understanding," but the Greek word is "kardia," from which we

get our English word, "cardiac." This doesn't just refer to man's intellectual understanding but it refers to "the eyes of the heart." We can't
forget that in the Bible, "heart" means every area and function of man's
personality. Paul uses a remarkable phrase in Ephesians 1:18: "the eyes
of your heart." So each believer has two pairs of eyes. One pair is in his
head, and the other pair is in his heart. But just like the eyes in his head
must be trained and developed after his biological birth so we can use
them properly, the eyes of his heart must be trained and developed as
well after the new birth. Our hearts have eyes by which we are to see
(all things) from the depths of our personality. But this seeing requires
spiritual illumination.

Paul reveals the source of this illumination of the heart in verse seventeen. He tells the Ephesians that he is praying for them, "That the
God of our Lord Jesus Christ, the Father of glory, may give unto you the
spirit of wisdom and revelation." "Wisdom" is the understanding and
appropriation of divine truth and then, "revelation" is the "unveiling," of
God and His truth. Why do you think they are in this order? You might
expect revelation to come first, then wisdom, but think about this: In
Genesis 1:3 God created light before He created the material universe.
Why do you suppose that is? Because, no matter how many worlds God
created, no matter how many eyes He made, there would have been no
sight without the light. The same thing is true in the spiritual experience. God gives wisdom with which to understand (this is the means to
see). Then, He begins to bring His revelation (the thing to see) before us
as we search for Him.

Paul also reveals the **subject of this illumination** in verse seventeen. The subject of our illumination is "the knowledge of Him." There
are some very important things about God here that we need to know
and understand. There are three kinds of knowledge. There is that

knowledge that we can call scientific knowledge; there is the knowledge that we call social knowledge; and then there is spiritual knowledge. The basic, ultimate, eternal knowledge is relational knowledge. That is our personal knowledge of God, ourselves, and then others. This is reflected in the "great commandment," the duty to "love God with all your heart, mind, soul, and strength," and the second great commandment, which is to "love your neighbor as yourself." The greatest knowledge of all is the knowledge of God through His Son, Jesus Christ. In fact, Jesus said, "This is life eternal, that they may know Thee, the only true God, and Jesus Christ, Whom Thou hast sent" (John 17:3 KJV). To know God personally is salvation; to know God progressively is sanctification; and to know God perfectly is glorification. A wise man once said, "Information is everywhere; but revelation or insight is all too rare."

Then we come to the most incredible part of Paul's prayer. Now we can begin to see why this matter of illumination is so vitally important for us. In verse eighteen Paul says that the ***purpose of illumination***, or this "heart seeing," is "that you may know." Paul says God wants us to know some things. The word "know" here is the Greek word "oida." This is not the word for our intellectual or academic knowing, the knowing you do by the use of your mind, your brain, your reason, or your intelligence. The word "oida" means "to know by seeing." This is the spiritual seeing of the heart, and it requires that the eyes of our heart be opened and flooded with divine light, which is a miracle of the Holy Spirit and when this occurs, a blind person can then say, "Oh, now I can see!" This is probably what Helen Keller was referring to when she said, "I would rather be blind the way I am blind, and see the way I see, than to see the way many people do, and be blind the way they are blind." A reporter asked Miss Keller once, "Is there anything worse than to be without organic sight?" She quickly replied, "Oh, yes, there is one thing much worse, and that is to have sight without vision." But remember, true vision is an absolute miracle of God!

What does the illumined person "know by seeing"? Verses eighteen and nineteen have been called "the prayer of the three what's." When the eyes of my heart are opened by a miracle of God, I discover some very important things. First of all, when the eyes of my heart are enlightened about who I am in Christ, I do not have to *protect* myself—because I discover that God has provided perfect *security* for me in Christ. Secondly, when the eyes of my heart are enlightened about who I am in Christ, I do not have to *prove* myself—because God has provided perfect *significance* for me; and when my heart is flooded with God's light, I do not have to *provide* for myself—because I know God has supplied perfect *sufficiency* for me.

These three "what's" are the three objects of this great prayer for illumination and they will solve the three greatest problems in a believer's life. Psalm 119:130 says, "The unfolding of Your words gives light; it gives understanding to the simple" (NASB). We have to ask God to make us simple! We need to ask Him for this simplicity of heart and spirit. We need to ask for the correct or proper entrance of His words into our minds and our hearts, and for the light that will enable us to see and appreciate these three incredible "what's." I pray regularly: Father, enlarge my capacity to know you and to hear from you today. God, flood my heart with your light today so that I might see things from your perspective.

Did you know that the telescope was accidentally discovered by a Dutch spectacle maker? Spectacle making involves handling lenses that are checked simply be looking through them. It was during an examination that the spectacle maker found himself looking through not one, but two lenses and to his surprise the magnification of the lens combination was much greater than that of a single lens. In placing the two lenses at opposite ends of a tube, the telescope was invented. The accident, mind you, happened to a careful and diligent researcher. 2 Timothy 2:15 says, "Study to show yourself approved unto God…"

When it comes to spiritual matters, the "serendipities," or those happy surprises (accidents?), happen to the diligent researchers. We have to be heart-hungry and we must be humble to experience them. John Baillie said, "I am sure that the bit of the road that most requires to be illuminated is the point where it forks." We sometimes do more damage in the community of believers because we rush ahead roughly and crudely, without illumination, at the forks of the road—the forks of doctrinal differences, etc. So we have to approach this great territory boldly, but humbly.

Paul is praying here that God may open the eyes of our hearts and flood them with light, so that we (Christians) may know by seeing "what is the hope of our calling." At a mere glance, these words sound so innocent, don't they? But once you look deeper, thoroughly and carefully studying, you see why the reader needs illumination. This is a vast treasure, dear heart, and we have to dig for treasure. There are two words that we should really pay close attention to here. One is the word "hope" and the other is the word "calling." These words do not mean in the New Testament what we mean when we use them in everyday conversation today. Today, a "calling" is an inviting. But in the New Testament, the word "calling" is the all-inclusive word for our divine salvation. So we see immediately that this first "what" is a lot bigger than it first appeared to be.

Then we have this awesome word, "hope." Again, the word is much bigger and more meaningful than even our big word "hope." To us, hope is wish-projection, or wishful thinking. It is the desire for something in the future. But in the New Testament, the word "hope" has greater dimension to it. It is identified in the New Testament as "a sure and certain hope." So this prayer is that the eyes of the believer's heart will be opened up and flooded with light, in order that we may know by seeing how absolutely guaranteed our salvation is! Beloved, think about this: It is God's intention that each believer would have absolute, unconditional, perfect assurance of his or her salvation. Do you see now why I said that as a believer, we no longer have to prove ourselves, because God has provided perfect, invulnerable, invincible security for us? Beloved, only secure people will ever really serve God! Insecure people cannot really serve God because they have to serve themselves, always seeking after that security that eludes them outside of Christ.

Every person outside of Christ is a nobody seeking to make of himself a somebody, but every person in Christ (though many don't know it) is everything to the most important Person in the universe; so, he can easily volunteer to be nothing, because he cannot lose what he has in Christ. Once he is truly in Christ, he is perfectly secure! So Paul's prayer in Ephesians is a petition that every born again believer will realize their perfect absolute security in Jesus Christ. But look around you. It is easy to see that most Christians (yes, truly born-again people) act regularly out of insecurity instead of security. We see it in the territorial Christianity; marginalizing others for personal safety! Why? Because the first "what" has never been deeply and richly illuminated to the eyes of their hearts. Is this an important prayer—or what?

Now, take that second "what" in Paul's prayer. Paul prays that the eyes of our hearts may be flooded with light, that we may "know by seeing what are the riches of the glory of His inheritance in the saints." What "inheritance" is he speaking of? Oh great God…we need to see this beloved! Our first tendency is to see this as the believer's inheritance.

But that cannot be what Paul is referring to. The believer's inheritance in Christ has already been dealt with in the preceding verses. Look back at Ephesians 1:11. No, the inheritance he is talking about here is God's inheritance in us. You see, Christ and His estate are the believer's inheritance. But, you (the Christian, the born again child of God) are "God's inheritance." Now, here is a key to finding true significance. Study the Old Testament, and you just take note of how many times our Father calls His people His "portion," or God's "lot," or God's "treasure," or God's "inheritance." This is the idea here. Christians are God's inheritance, God's treasure! From God's viewpoint, He came into possession of something extremely valuable when He saved you! So what did God get when He got you? Can you believe it? God says that He got rich! Paul speaks of the "riches of the glory of His inheritance in the saints." You, dear Christian, are God's portion, God's lot, God's precious treasure. You are unbelievably valuable to Him!

Now, most of you are thinking right now to yourselves, "You have got to be kidding! The God who would become rich by getting me must not have much by way of inventory." But again, we have to put on the spiritual lenses of heaven. We have to think with the mind of God. We have to see with the eyes of Christ. This is huge, people! We are talking about worth from God's point of view. Every Christian on earth is worth the exact equivalent in value to Jesus Christ Himself—that is in God's eyes. How do we know that? Because that is exactly what God paid for us—Jesus Christ Himself! Now, none of us could make the claim that we are inherently equal in value to Jesus.

We have to understand that the value referred to here is a conferred value, not mere inherent value. God confers onto you and me this value. Let me explain. Suppose that I am very, very rich. Then suppose that you own a grocery store and I walk into your store one day and say, "I want to buy a Classic Coke and I am prepared to pay you twelve million dollars for it." What would you do? Why, you'd offer me a case or more, if you were a savvy store owner. Ha! Well, as silly as that illustration may be, it helps us to see a massive, vital truth. The value of an article is not determined by the price tag on it. The value of something is determined by the willingness and capability of the one who wants to make the purchase. "Who is a deposit guaranteeing our inheritance until the redemption of those who are God's possession—to the praise of his glory" (Ephesians 1:14), and it refers to the believer as God's "purchased possession," and verse seven tells us that the price of purchase was the life, the death, the blood, of Jesus Christ Himself. So God has placed on every Christian the exact value of Jesus Christ Himself. Now beloved, that is a Wow! moment.

There is a painting entitled *Irises* by Vincent van Gogh and that painting sold for $53.9 million. The canvas and paint alone were barely worth ten dollars by today's standards, yet Alan Bond, an Australian financier, was willing to pay an incredible price for that work of art. Pretty incredible, isn't it? Well, would you think any differently of yourself if someone very famous and important regarded you as a treasure of incalculable value, like a great work of art, a masterpiece? Dear one that is exactly what God says you are! Let me repeat, "What God says and sees matters". Ephesians 2:10 says that "We are His workmanship, created in Christ Jesus...." We are Father's work of art, His masterpiece, His featured attraction. Beloved, our God is crazy about us! If that doesn't clear up some feelings of insecurity, you had better check your pulse to see if there is a heartbeat!

Now I am talking about grace or conferred worth here. And, here's the clincher. Get ready. God confers onto you and to me the very value of Jesus Christ himself by the purchase of Calvary and then, in order to justify His investment, God sets out immediately after our salvation to make us like Jesus. Stop! Go back! Read that previous sentence again. Did you get it? Did you? If that is not a Wow! moment, I don't know what is. That just rocks my world. Do you see why we don't have to prove ourselves any longer? Our great God has provided us with perfect significance through Christ and Calvary. We are His cherished treasure! So this prayer is a petition that every one of His "born agains" will realize our personal significance is found in Christ. He is crazy about us! He is crazy in love with me and I am crazy in love with Him! This is a crazy kind of love. I don't fully understand it. But I fully embrace it. I totally believe everything Jesus says about the matter and I thank God for it. So Paul's prayer is a prayer that God will flood our hearts with light, so that we will "know by seeing;" so we will understand our incredible worth to God and to His Kingdom.

Finally, I want you to consider the final "what" of Paul's prayer in Ephesians. He says, "I pray that the eyes of your heart might be flooded with light; that you may know by seeing, "What is the exceeding greatness of God's power toward us who believe." So here is the third "what" of this prayer and it has to do with our personal sufficiency. It has to do with God's power in our lives. Ephesians 3:20 is one of my favorite verses: "Now to him who is able to do immeasurably more than all we ask or imagine, according to his power that is at work within us." Paul is talking here about God's power within us. It is *defined power* (verse 19) and it is a *demonstrated power* (verses 20-23). This defines God's power as something that is active and operating in our daily lives. One word for power in verse 19 is the Greek word, "dunamis," and this is where we get our English word "dynamic." This word essentially means capability or potential. Wow...we've got dynamite living inside of us! However, we need to understand that they could not have been talking about dynamite. Dynamite was not invented until 1866 by Alfred Nobel. The Greeks did not know about dynamite. So, more likely, they were speaking of a "dynamic" power.

This dynamic power of God is explosive and always is intended to have an outward expansive result. The result should be an outward (others focused) movement in our lives, exemplifying God's power. Not a boom power, but a blessing power. God is always about advancement and enlargement of space. "*Enlarge* the place of your tent, *stretch* your tent curtains wide, do not hold back; *lengthen* your cords, *strengthen* your stakes (Isaiah 54:2). God is always at work in our lives and He always desires that we go farther and deeper with Him in intimacy and impact. But, our outreach will always be in proportion to our depth. You will never go farther until you have gone deeper. This dunamis power is at work in us to produce a product for God's glory and praise.

A second word for power is verse nineteen is the word "energeia," which gives us our words "energy" and "energize." This word means effective or operational power. Then, there is a third word and it is the Greek word "kratos," and it refers to power that is exercised in resistance or control. And the final word is "ischuos," which indicates inherent, vital power. So again, Paul overflows with words to show us how great this character dynamic is and to also show us that it is available to every believer in Christ.

But Paul doesn't stop here. He doesn't stop with just words that define God's power. He also points to certain events that demonstrate God's power. Get this: When the Bible wants to impress us with the love of God, it points us to the cross. But, when the Bible wants to impress us with the power of God, it points us to the resurrection and exaltation of Christ. Paul concludes his prayer by praising God's power:

Which he wrought in Christ, when he raised him from the dead, and set him at his own right hand in the heavenly places, Far above all principality, and power, and might, and dominion, and every name that is named, not only in this world, but also in that which is to come: And hath put all things under his feet, and gave him to be the head over all things to the church, Which is his body, the fullness of him that fills all in all. (Ephesians 1:20-23 KJV)

So He declares that the same power that elevated Jesus to a position of glory is available to elevate us to a life of divine sufficiency. Praise God! That is enough to make me take off and have a *"runnin' shoutin' fit!"* Let me make an important emphasis on something though. This power, this dynamic power, this vital, energizing power is available to us for the sake of building our character and exerting that spiritual character impact upon others. That power is the same resurrecting power today. God can resurrect dead relationships, broken marriages and any other dead thing. Do you see why I said earlier that I do not have to *provide* for myself—because God has supplied perfect sufficiency for me?

But, we have to admit that these truths are foreign to most Christians. And we only have to guess that one of the primary reasons for this lack of power is a lack of spiritual illumination. This is why it is so important to remember this. "What you see is what you will be"—within the limits of God's revealed truth. What you behold lovingly, longingly and lastingly, you will become like! We need to behold Jesus and just keep on beholding Him! Do you see why this is the most important prayer that any Christian can pray for another? By this prayer of the three "what's" and the answer to them, the problems of insecurity, insignificance, and insufficiency are solved for every believer. The psalmist said to God, "In Thy light shall we see light" (Psalm 36:9) and "The unfolding of Your words gives light; it gives understanding to the simple" (Psalm 119:130 NASB).

As God gives us the grace to see with spiritual eyes, His story becomes ours, His vision becomes ours, His concerns become ours, and His vocation becomes ours. So illumination is a continual necessity in the believer's life if we are going to have any true significant impact for Christ.

Lord, you have given sufficient sight at our new birth; now, please Lord, give us sufficient light! Open our hearts and flood them with light so that we might truly see just how incredible you are and how big your plan is for each one of your children. Enlarge our capacity to see it, Father, and to move upward and outward with a greater spiritual impact on others; all for your sake Lord Jesus and for your glory. I pray this in the matchless name of Jesus, because you said that I could. Amen!

CHAPTER SIX

What Did You Bring To Put It In?

And he spoke many things to them in parables,
saying, Behold the sower went out to sow; and
as he sowed, some seeds fell beside the road, and
the birds came and ate them up. Others fell on the
rocky places, where they did not have much soil,
and immediately they sprang up, because they had
no depth of soil. But when the sun had risen, they
were scorched; and because they had no root they
withered away. Others fell among the thorns, and
the thorns came up and choked them out. And
others fell on good soil and yielded a crop, some a
hundredfold, some sixty, some thirty. He who has
ears to hear, let him hear.   —Matthew 13:3-9

What do you think Jesus talked about more than anything else? If you
could answer me I know I would hear a variety of answers. Some would
say that Jesus spoke about heaven more than anything else, or perhaps
hell, or money, or love. There would be a multitude of answers and likely
not the correct one. Jesus talked about a lot of things. He talked a lot
about love and forgiveness and he talked about giving and many other
things. Are you ready for this? More than just about anything else, Jesus

talked about hearing. He talked about our listening or lack thereof. In the parable of the sower in Luke chapter eight and in Matthew chapter thirteen, Jesus interpreted that parable as a message about hearing. Sixteen times in eleven verses Jesus used some form of the verb to hear, and then He made a crazy statement. He said, "Let him who has ears to hear, let him hear." What exactly did Jesus mean by that? Well, He meant there is hearing and then there is *hearing*. My husband is the poster boy for this! We laugh about it all the time. He says he would have to admit that his hearing becomes very selective when I'm speaking to him especially concerning his honey-do list. Well, according to Jesus, our hearing is always in question and it is vitally important that we correct our hearing problems, especially if we are going to have the maximum impact for Christ.

Listen one more time: Jesus said, "He, who hath ears…": This is a person's *capacity* to hear. Then, he says, "to hear…": This is a person's *opportunity* to hear. And finally he says, "let him hear…": This is a person's *responsibility* to hear." Compare this to the Greek text, in which "to hear" translates a present active infinitive—which means "to hear." This is obviously a parable about hearing. Let me repeat: Sixteen times in some eleven verses in the text and context, Jesus referred to hearing. So, this is very important. I have many times heard people say after hearing God's Word preached or taught by an anointed speaker, that they just did not get anything out of the message. I have often thought how strange it is that we come to hear a man or woman teach or preach and fully expect them to be prayed up, studied up, and anointed. But, somehow we think it is less important that we ourselves, the hearers, come prepared, prayed up and with anointed ears to hear from God. Our spiritual hearing is crucial (literally, "cross-serious") in its importance.

Each born again person has four ears—two on his head and two in his heart. Just like we have four eyes after we are saved, we had two when we were born, then we got two more when we were born again. A person may have 20/20 vision—perfect vision physically and yet be stone cold dead in the eyes of his heart simply because he has never been born again. So he has only his natural hearing and natural sight with which to perceive things, and appraise things. But Jesus said, "I tell you the truth, no one can see the Kingdom of God unless he is born again" (John 3:3 NIV). Jesus did not say, "You will not go to heaven." He said you cannot *see* the Kingdom of heaven. So our hearing and our seeing are very important in the Christian life. This is a big concept and a needed understanding in the Christian faith.

In Herb Hodges book, *Fox Fever*, he makes this assessment, and I agree: "From the moment of conversion, the new believer is expected to maintain a student attitude throughout his remaining life on earth." (We are always to be learning). He says, "Thus, the very vocation of the believer is to "learn to learn" It is amazing to note how many college graduates were never taught somewhere along the way how to study and how to learn. I believe it's a matter of being a good listener. Most Christians today are so oriented to auditing lessons in Sunday school and auditing sermons in an auditorium that they unwittingly abort the intention of Heaven for communication of truth. Note the take-off on the word "listening," which typically ends with the *moment* of listening and has no future productivity beyond that moment—which means that, when the staggering potential is considered for future productivity through such a moment, God largely wasted His breath in speaking in that service.

As we traffic through this parable in Matthew chapter thirteen, I want to remind you of something. You have heard it said that a parable is a heavenly story with an earthly meaning. But, it is really much more than that. A parable is a handle that Jesus puts into our hands to enable us to pick up a truth and take it home with us. This truth can and will change the way you look at God's Word, the living seed. We normally call this story "the parable of the sower." But, it seems to be told more as an analysis of the soil-types more than an assessment of the sower. So, it could easily be called "the parable of the soils." However, verse nine gives us an excellent key for interpreting the parable. This parable is about our hearing. What people hear when they are confronted with the truth of God is determined by the spiritual sensitivity of their heart. The seed represented is the Word of God and the soil is the heart of man. We need divine revelation and spiritual illumination from God to really get what's here. Divine revelation and illumination are not required for us to see farmers sowing their seed out in their fields in the springtime. But, it is the spiritual message of the parable that requires divine revelation and illumination.

The first prominent feature in the parable is the soils. There are four different "levels" of the seed's penetration into the various kinds of soils in the story. These four levels of penetration represent different levels of our listening or hearing, or they can represent different levels of cooperation with the truth heard. In the first case, the seed was *on* the soil, but not *in* it. In the second case, the seed was *on* the soil, and *in* it, but it could not get *down*. In the third case, the seed was *on*, *in* and *down*, but it could not get back *up*. In the final case, the seed was *on*, *in*, *down*, *up* and *out*. You need to keep the word *out* stored in the forefront of your mind. Because that word *out* pictures the result that God always desires from us whenever we hear His word in regards to penetration. The action and its result is always to be *outward*! The kind of Christianity we see most of the time is implosive (outside-in) rather than inside-out.

We see it in crowds of Christians regularly gathering into meeting places. Jesus mandated the outward, outgoing manifestation of the gospel. You see; the church building should be the base for Christian movement, not the place of the Christian movement.

In the story, the human heart is like soil, and the message of the Kingdom is like seed. And in this parable every listener discriminates in his listening, filtering the truth that is "sown" on the soil of his or her heart by preconceptions and preoccupations. The first kind of hearing is represented by the much-trodden wayside soil. This represents the *solid*-hearted listener. This person's heart is so closed and hardened that there is zero penetration of the gospel. When the seed strikes this kind of soil, it can't penetrate, so it just lies vulnerable on the surface and the birds (the enemy) detect it and quickly devour it. This type of soil represents the listener who really thinks the gospel is "for the birds"! Beloved, it's dangerous for us to attend church, treat the truth we hear with glib indifference, and make no serious response to the demands of that truth.

The second kind of listening is symbolized in the story by the *shallow soil*. Jesus is describing a terrain where a sub-surface shelf of rock is covered by a thin layer of topsoil. The seed had "no depth of earth," and so it could not get beyond just a quick show of life. "When the sun was up, the new plants were scorched; and because they had no root, they withered away." This soil represents the *shallow*-hearted listener. This is that listener who is very enthusiastic and receptive at first. But, when the real terms of discipleship and the Kingdom begin to fully dawn on him, and persecution and trouble are thrown into the mix, he quickly turns back to his old self-centered ways.

The third kind of listening is symbolized by *thorn*-infested soil. This is the strangled or suffocated listener. The plant would bear fruit, but it gets choked out by the thick thorns which infest this soil as the plant tries to come up from the earth. These thorns, according to Jesus, represent "the cares of this world, the deceitfulness of riches, and the lusts of other things entering in," and those competing interests choke the Word, and it becomes unfruitful.

The fourth kind of listening is symbolized by the good soil. This is the *spiritual* listener. This kind of listener bears fruit unto God. We must be careful here, because there is no truly "spiritual" listener who *does not* bear fruit for God—on His terms. "So, my brothers, you also died to the law through the body of Christ, that you might belong to another, to him who was raised from the dead, in order that we might bear fruit to God" (Romans 7:4). This is receptive of well cultivated soil. This is a listener, learner and follower of Jesus Christ, otherwise known as a disciple of Christ.

Our listening is always in question. Two English women were talking at a Christian convention in London. One said, "I'm from Birmingham, and I am privileged every Sunday to hear the great Dr. John Henry Jowett." The other lady protested, "My dear; that is not a privilege; that is a fearful responsibility!" You see, hearing gospel truth is a great joy for the Christian, but listening to the gospel is not just for our pleasure; it's more for spiritual productivity. God's intention is always for His truth to produce much fruit in our lives. Are we hearing and then producing? Two men were conversing. One asked casually, "Does your wife ever talk to herself?" The other replied smugly, "Yes, she does, but she doesn't know it—she thinks I'm listening!" When God speaks, He doesn't intend to talk to Himself. He has enlisted our capacity to hear, and He makes us responsible for listening. "He who has ears to hear, let him hear." Our hearing is vitally important!

Basil Matthews, a great English preacher, came annually years ago to the Calvary Baptist Church in New York City for a Bible conference.

One year, he shared the program with an Indian preacher from the western United States. The two developed a friendship during their week of service together. One afternoon, they were walking down a busy street toward their hotel. Sounds of the subway, elevated trains, cars, and people saturated their ears. Suddenly the Indian preacher stopped on the sidewalk, placed his hand on Matthews' shoulder to arrest his steps, and exclaimed, "I hear a cricket!" After a moment, he walked rapidly to the street corner and crossed to the far side of the street. They were in front of a flower shop. The Indian entered the shop with Matthews hurrying curiously behind. The Indian listened a moment inside the shop, walked over to a series of potted plants on a shelf, thrust in his hand, and pulled out a cricket. The amazed Matthews walked admiringly with him out of the store. Once outside, he remarked, "That's absolutely amazing. How do you do that?" The Indian replied, "My friend, I learned a long time ago that people hear what they want to hear. Let me show you." He reached in his pocket, pulled out two half-dollars, and threw them down on the sidewalk. Instantly, four people changed their direction and dashed toward the money. The question is not, "Does God speak?" The question is, "Do we truly listen?" Do you listen to Father? Do you hear the Holy Spirit when He speaks to you? Do you listen openly, submissively, longingly, and most importantly, productively?

One Sunday morning, Alexander Whyte, the great Edinburgh pastor, preached a penetrating sermon about sin and its consequences. He didn't know it, but a mother and her college-age son were seated on the back pew in church that morning. The boy was home from college for the weekend. The next week, Dr. Whyte received two letters on different days. One was from the mother, and in the letter she blasted the pastor for his hard and condemning hellfire preaching. A day or so later, a letter came from the woman's son, who was back at college, and wrote to tell Dr. Whyte that he had been saved through his message on the past Sunday! To some listeners, the gospel produces a progression of "life unto life," while to others, it leads to "death unto death." Everything depends on the depth and quality of a person's listening. Beloved, at what level, with what intensity, with what awareness, with what outcome, do you listen to the Lord? When the preacher preaches, whose voice do you hear—his, or God's?

Another prominent feature in the story is the *seed*. The seed represents God's message, God's voice. Luke 8:11 says, "The seed is the Word of God." Think about a tiny little seed. A tiny seed can represent the apparent frailty of the truth of God. Any word seems frail and helpless, and this seems to be especially true of God's truth. You can take most seeds and hold them between your thumb and your index finger—and they will be hidden from sight. You can rub your finger and thumb together in a grinding motion—and they may disintegrate. James Russell Lowell admitted in his famous poem that truth is easily "crushed to earth." That which is frail to appearance has an unbelievable actual force.

Here is some amazing proof of this truth. In 1922, English archaeologist Howard Carter was excavating and studying in the Valley of the Kings in Central Egypt, when he cleared a work area inside a tomb and discovered that it had a false back wall. When he broke through that false wall, he found a new compartment, and that new compartment proved to be King Tut's tomb. The best of the contents of Tut's tomb are on display in the Cairo Museum. Among the many items found in the tomb, a metal urn filled with seeds was discovered. Remember that this tomb was approximately 3200 years old when discovered. The urn was opened and some of the seeds inside were sent to London for experimentation. A portion of the seeds were planted—and a garden full of plants came up from seeds which had lain dormant for over 3000 years!

You see, the gospel always has a vital and revitalizing power within it! Socialists are calling our age "the post-Christian era"—and the real reason is that God's people are not covering "the field" (Matthew 13:38) with the seeds of the Word of God (Luke 8:11). The divine life-germ inside the Word of God just needs to be planted in good soil, the soil of some divinely—prepared human heart, and a harvest with limitless potential will emerge. But, I'm afraid we suffer from "Gospel Overload." We have created inside the church a "Bible Lite—much taste, less filling." Hearing the Word over and over but not heeding the Word produces terminal intake of the gospel, instead of germinal planting of the gospel, the kind of planting that would produce a spiritual harvest. The truth you hear will either terminate with you or it will germinate with you, allowing the potential for infinite future harvests. What will you do with what you have heard?

The next time you go to hear God's precious Word preached or taught, make sure you take something to put it in. Make sure you are prepared to hear from God as much as you expect the speaker to be anointed to speak. We desperately need to learn that we are accountable for what we hear. And truth, that living seed of the Word of God, will do one of those two things. It will terminate with you or it will germinate in you and produce fruit for God's glory. The intended purpose for truth in our lives is to bear fruit for someone else's spiritual benefit. Our Christian life is to be lived with others in mind. God did not save you and me to get *us* out of *earth* into *heaven*. God saved us so that *He* could get out of *heaven* into *earth*. He wants to live his life in and through you and me. When we hear God speak, we must obey! When Jesus said, "Go and make disciples…," He was not just talking to hear himself talk. He was and is serious about our personal involvement in the Great Commission. Hearing His Word is a privilege and yet it is also an awesome responsibility.

Remember: The Christian life is Christ—Christ received by me, Christ resident in me, Christ reigning over me, Christ reproduced in me, Christ released through me, and Christ realized in others because of me. That's "inside-out" living. That's the disciple's lifestyle.

I have another "tulip moment" in regard to our listening to God's voice and obeying. Discerning God's voice and obeying him is vital to an abundant life—victorious life in Christ. I am always amazed at just how intimate Jesus wants to be with His children. The rewards always out-weigh the challenge to just listen and to obey. I must confess that, like most women, I like to shop. I like pretty things, remember? It has been a challenge to cultivate this intimate relationship with Jesus even to the degree of praying about my purchases and about what clothing I wear. Could Father really be at all interested in what we wear or how we look? Oh, yes, beloved, He is interested in every detail of our lives.

Recently, I was out with two of my primary Timothias and we were shopping at one of our favorite boutiques and I spotted the most beautiful blouse I had ever seen. I am telling you girls, it was a wow blouse! Of course you know what I mean. This blouse belonged in my closet. It was a Cheri Holcomb blouse. I thought, "I just have to have that blouse." That is, until I looked at the price tag. I knew the answer was, "No way!" It was way out of my price range. So, I just did some window shopping that day disappointed about the blouse. But all the way home that blouse was still on my mind. The next day I had a lunch meeting with two staff members from a local church for a planning meeting for an upcoming disciple-makers conference they were hosting. A dear friend of ours who was a member of the church also joined us for lunch and we had some wonderful fellowship. Our conversation was all about Jesus.

After the meeting, my friend came over to me as we were leaving and held out two one hundred dollar bills and said, "I want you to have this. God just told me to give it to you and I don't want you to spend it on bills or groceries, but I want you to spend it on you! Go buy something pretty for yourself." Well, I was just shocked and of course overjoyed. And you know exactly where I was headed! I went straight to that little boutique and bought that beautiful blouse for myself, and some earrings and necklace to boot! I was so excited. I just knew this blouse was the bomb and I was going to be so pretty in it.

As soon as I got home I pulled the blouse out of the shopping bag and put it on and stood in front of the mirror to admire it and suddenly the Holy Spirit said to my heart: "You didn't even ask Me if you could have that blouse. You didn't even ask Me if I liked it." Oh my, I was immediately embarrassed that I had grieved the Holy Spirit by excluding Him all together. I took the blouse off, put it back in the shopping bag and said, "Lord Jesus, I am so sorry that I didn't ask your opinion on the blouse and if you don't want me to have it, Lord, I will take it back." The silence was my obvious answer and so the next morning I returned the blouse and the earrings and the necklace to boot! Not only did I return the items that I had purchased but Father told me clearly what I was to do with that money. And let me just say it was not about me getting either a new blouse or anything else for myself. I had plenty of blouses. Now, I am not saying that we are never supposed to shop and get new clothes. That is not at all the point. I am talking about intimacy with God here. I am talking about walking in the Spirit, so I don't fulfill the lusts of my flesh.

Several months passed and one afternoon just a few weeks before Christmas, I met another precious friend and disciple for lunch. When I joined Melissa at the restaurant, she immediately pulled out a beautifully wrapped box with a giant red ribbon around it. I was so surprised. Melissa had a huge smile across her face. She is that friend who loves to give gifts and, well, I am that friend that loves to receive them! Ha-ha. I carefully removed the gift wrap, both us smiling from ear to ear. And when I pulled back the tissue paper, I could not believe my eyes. It was that blouse! It was that very same blouse. Melissa was God's messenger of reward that day for my act of love and obedience. I was simply overwhelmed with God's love for me and shared with Mel what I had done. We both just rejoiced in God's goodness. I tell you; God loves to send us presents. He loves to show us how deep and how wide his love goes.

Father, I love you and I praise you for your great love for me. Thank you that you care about every detail of our lives. Help me to press in closer to you. Help me to enthrone Jesus in every part of my life. You are worthy Lord!

CHAPTER SEVEN

Hanging With Jesus

"I am the true vine, and my Father is the vine-dresser. Every branch in Me that does not bear fruit He takes away: and every branch that bears fruit, He prunes it, that it may bear more fruit. You are already clean because of the word, which I have spoken to you. Abide in Me, and I in you. As the branch cannot bear fruit of itself, unless it abides in the vine; so neither can you, unless you abide in Me. I am the vine you are the branches. He who abides in me, and I in him, he bears much fruit; for apart from Me, you can do nothing. If anyone does not abide in Me, he is thrown away as a branch, and dries up; and men gather them, and cast them into the fire, and they are burned. If you abide in Me, and my words abide in you, ask what you wish, and it shall be done for you. By this is my Father glorified, that you bear much fruit; and so prove to be My disciples. Just as the Father has loved me, so have I loved you: abide in my love. If you keep my commandments, you will abide in my love; just as I have kept my Father's commandments, and abide in his love. These things I have spoken to you, that My joy may be in you, and that your joy may be made full."
—John 15:1-11 NASB

As I continue on this faith journey and I strive for the ever-enlarging presence and power of Christ to be evident in and through my life, I want to reproduce His life in others. In order to do that, I must understand the simplicity of the abiding life in Christ. I cannot live the Christian life, only Christ can live His life in and through me. I heard about a young man who met Billy Graham once and upon their meeting, Mr. Graham asked the young man, "How are you doing?" and the young man replied, "Well, I'm just trying to live the Christian life," to which Mr. Graham replied, "Well, have you ever tried to be an elephant?" We cannot live His life. Jesus must live His own life in and through us. It truly is a life of abiding. I like to call it just hanging with Jesus. As I live to make disciples, I pray that this is evident in my walk, that I abide in Him, therefore, He brings forth the fruit!

One of the key words of the Bible and of the Christian life is the word "new." The Bible talks about how we can receive a new heart and a new spirit. It speaks of us becoming a new creature in Christ and of the new covenant in Him, of the new birth, of being a new man, and having a new life. There will be a New Jerusalem, and it speaks of many other wonderful new things. In John chapter fifteen, we have one of the last messages that Jesus gave to His disciples before His death on the cross. Here we have an answer to the unstated question, "What's new for a Christian?" There are many things that I have as a Christian that I did not have before.

In this passage, Jesus uses an illustration from nature. In the illustration, He tells us that the Christian life is a matter of relationship, and not of rules or regulations or religious ritual. The Christian life simply involves a personal relationship between two persons, Jesus Christ and the individual believer. The illustration He uses is one of the vine and its branches. He declares that He is the vine, and that the Christian is a branch in the vine. Just like the vine and its branches have an inner relationship in which the inner sap of the vine flows through the branch and gives it life, the Christian should have a vibrant life-receiving relationship with Jesus Christ, and this relationship should be regarded and treasured as an absolute essential to the believer's life.

In these verses, Jesus tells us some things that are new for a Christian. There are at least four new things that a Christian has simply because he is a Christian. As we discover these truths, we become more useful to our Master. We become more fruitful for His glory! When we become Christians we are first of all given a new *position* in Christ. When you and I got saved, we experienced the "Great Exchange." We stepped out of ourselves into everything that Jesus is. Six times in the first seven verses of John fifteen, Jesus used the phrase, "in Me," and He used that phrase to describe this new position we have as Christians. It is interesting to note that the preposition "in" is used by Jesus about thirty times in the fourteenth and fifteenth chapters of the Gospel of John. Then Jesus couples it with the personal pronoun "me." The Christian is "in Christ." When you read the later books of the New Testament, you find the phrase, "in Christ," occurring over and over again. In fact, just in Paul's letters alone, the phrase "in Christ" is used 164 times to define the Christian's new position.

We really need to understand the massive truth of this tiny phrase. Here is one of those truths so easily mishandled or easily overlooked. Once we truly understand this it becomes the joy, the power, and the very assurance of the Christian life. I believe that the two most important words ever combined together are the words "in Christ." These two words reveal the uniqueness of Jesus and our relationship with Him. We could never imagine thinking of ourselves as "in Abe Lincoln," or "in Napoleon Bonaparte," or "in" any other renowned person of recent history. But any practicing Christian should be increasingly comfortable with the phrase "in Christ." Jesus Himself introduced this idea in our text here in John chapter fifteen. So, Jesus gives us a little key that opens a very large door, just a preposition and a proper name, but what an idea! So that we can better understand this phrase, just contrast our new position "in Christ" with our old position before we trusted in Christ. First Corinthians 15:22 says, "For as is Adam all die, so in Christ all will be made alive." Note the two prepositional phrases, "in Adam" and "in Christ." Every person on earth is seen by God in one of two possible positions.

There are only two representative men of history, Adam and Christ. Every person is represented by one of these men, and it is very much a matter of *position*. You are either in Adam or in Christ. To be "in Adam" means that you fell into sin when Adam fell into sin, you became lost when Adam became lost, and came under the judgment of God when Adam came under the judgment of God—a matter of position. So the most important thing about you is your position. If you have never had a real and radical change of position, you are still "in Adam" and that means you are not a Christian. Second Corinthians 5:17 says, "Therefore if any man is *in Christ*, he is a new creature; old things passed away; behold, new things have come" (NASB). Romans 8:1 says, "Therefore, there is now no condemnation for those who are *in Christ* Jesus." The key phrase in both of these crucial verses is the phrase, "in Christ."

Mark Twain once wrote a short story about an old slave who lived on a narrow peninsula of land that jutted out into the Mississippi River from the mother body of the state of Missouri. Each evening after work, he would leave the plantation and go to his small hut on the peninsula. During the spring of one year, when the river was flooding beyond its banks, a powerful swirling eddy of water cut through the upper arm of the peninsula one night and severed it from its connection with the state of Missouri. The peninsula was now an island. But the law said that when it was severed from Missouri, it automatically and immediately became a part of the state of Illinois across the river. But here's the impact of the story: the state of Missouri was a slave state, while Illinois was a free state. So that man went to bed one night a slave, and awakened the next day a free man—and he didn't even know it! What made the difference? Only one thing—his position.

Can you imagine that former slave's feelings when he was told that he was now free for the first time in his life? Can you imagine the bewilderment as he spends the rest of his life trying to adjust to his freedom after living his entire life as a slave? It is the same way with a Christian. He has spent his entire life in Adam and is fully adjusted to that position. Then, one day, he is transplanted out of Adam into Christ. He must then spend the rest of his life discovering the meaning, the resources, and the responsibilities of his new position. He is now surrounded by Christ, separated unto Christ, sheltered in Christ, and supplied by Christ. But suppose his mentality still retains only the awareness of his old position in Adam. How important it is for the Christian to discover from the Word of God everything that it means to be "in Christ"?

Not only do we have a new position in Christ, secondly, this passage tells us that we have a new possession in life as a Christian. In John 15:4, Jesus uses another innocent-sounding little phrase that opens up vast riches and resources to the Christian. The phrase is, "I in you." The "I" is Jesus, and the "you" is the Christian. Christ is in the Christian. In verse five, speaking of the believer, Jesus said, "I (am) in him." What an awesome thought! Jesus Christ is literally living inside of me! Jesus is in every Christian. "A Christ not in you, is a Christ not yours." Isn't this what the New Testament constantly teaches? In John 1:12, the Bible says, "But as many as received Him, to them He gave the right to become children of God" (NASB). In Colossians 1:27, the Bible speaks of "Christ in you, the hope of glory." In Galatians 2:20, the Apostle Paul said, "Christ lives in me." Indeed, the Presence of the indwelling Christ is the test of salvation and eternal life. In 1 John 5:12, the Apostle John wrote, "He that hath the Son hath life, but he that hath not the Son of God hath not life" (KJV). You see, Jesus Christ actually lives inside a born-again believer in Jesus Christ. It is a strange combination of new things: I am "in Christ" and Christ is in me. How can this be? You can take a sponge and see this truth illustrated. Put the sponge in the water and ask yourself this question. Is the water in the sponge or is the sponge in the water? Both are true. I am in Christ and He is in me.

A bird flies through the air. The bird is in the air, and the air is in the bird. Take a cold bar of iron and put it in a hot fire. The iron is in the fire, and in a few minutes the fire is in the iron. In fact, if you were to touch the bar of iron after it had been in the fire for some time, you wouldn't quietly say, "That's a bar of iron." You would exclaim, "That's hot!" and you would adjust quickly to that fact. Even so, when a lost sinner is around a spiritual Christian, he should receive immediate impressions and reminders of the Person dwelling within him, the Lord Jesus Christ. There is nothing forced about this impression, and it may take the observer some time to be aware of it.

So the real secret of the Christian life is that Somebody Else is living in the Christian, desiring to reproduce His life in terms of the personality of the individual in whom He dwells. I love to use this truth as a witness and have had some wonderful opportunities to do so. I learned this too from it being modeled in another's life.

Lee and I attended a wedding and at the reception we were seated at a table with three other couples. I am always quick to make friends and so I sparked conversation as soon as we were seated. One of the ladies seated next to me was easily engaged and we were off to get to know one another a little. After a few minutes of "How many children do you have?" and "What do you do for a living?," she asked me to accompany her to the bar for another glass of wine. I agreed and while we were standing at the bar waiting she asked if she could get me a glass of wine also. I said with a smile, "No thanks; I have somebody else living inside of me, and I have already checked with Him and He doesn't have a taste for it." She replied with a somewhat confused look upon her face, "Oh, you do? Well, I want you to know that I don't drink to get drunk, I just enjoy the buzz." I said, "Really? I used to drink before Jesus saved me and when I did drink, I must confess, I did it to get drunk..." and on I went into a brief testimony about how Jesus had saved me. We casually walked back to our table and continued a long while with the normal chit-chat, and at the end of the evening as Lee and I were saying our good nights, this woman leaned over to me, handed me her business card with her phone number and asked if we could possibly get together some other time to discuss further this one who now was living inside of me and obviously meant so much to me. I was so excited! It just seemed so easy to "fling that seed." Because of my position in Christ and my new possession of Him in Me, I have this confidence. He can live His life through me!

Jesus wants His life to burst out of us. What a startling fact! I have the Person who created all things (Colossians 1:16), and who holds all things together (Colossians 1:17), actually living in me. We need to ponder this question carefully: If Jesus Christ is literally in me, isn't that by far the most significant fact of my life? We need to stop and really get our heads around this. Because of this fact, I have the very mind of Christ (1 Corinthians 2:16). I am a living vessel (2 Timothy 2:21, 2 Corinthians

4:7). What is a vessel? A vessel is an object, a container that is created and intended to contain someone or something else. We were created to house or contain Him, His *Presence*. Why? For what purpose did Jesus come into me? He did not come in to replace me, in which case I would lose my identity. He came in to regenerate me, to renew me, and to release His personality through me. There is to be ongoing communion between Him and me on a consistent basis. You see, Jesus has truly, fully, and perfectly lived the Christian life. I cannot live that life (His life) without Him. God would never expect me to live that impossibility. That's the reason He came into me, to do in me and for me, by a grace and faith cooperation, what I simply cannot do without Him.

Yet since He came in, I now have a powerful *Performer* within me, and He is willing, eager, and able to unite Himself and all of His resources with my poor life. Galatians 2:20 says, "I have been crucified with Christ and I no longer live, but Christ lives in me. The life I live in the body, I live by faith in the Son of God, who loved me and gave himself for me." If Jesus is mine, then all His resources are mine. This means, daringly, that I have the personality potential of Jesus Christ Himself— except for my sins, and the fact that I am not Jesus. This is the reason God must deal so severely with my sins—to remove that which violates and destroys me, and to remove the margin of difference between me and full likeness to Jesus.

So the Christian life is a matter of appropriating by faith the *Person* and resources that are in me. I have come to understand that as a born again believer, I am a container of the very presence, power and essence of God. I am also a carrier of that presence and power and essence and ultimately I am to be a conveyor of the life of God for others to see and to respond to. Now we can begin to see what the strategy of Satan is likely to be with regard to a Christian. Satan will do everything in his ability to keep a Christian ignorant of his new position and his new possession, or he will do everything he can to neutralize the Christian's use of these things. He wants us to be like the lady who died of malnutrition with over a million dollars of currency in her home. She had the resources, but she wasn't "cashing in" her benefits. She had a possession she wasn't using. As a Christian, I have Jesus Christ living within me. Am I maximizing His presence there? Are you maximizing His presence there?

Not only does the born again believer have a *new position* and a *new possession*, thirdly, a Christian has a *new product* in life. Six times in the first eight verses of John fifteen, Jesus used the word "fruit." Then in verse five, He said, "I am the vine; you are the branches. If a man remains in me and I in him, he will bear much fruit; apart from me you can do nothing." This is to be the new product of the Christian's life. We are to bear fruit, or as Paul described it in Romans 7:4, "Fruit unto God." The Scripture reveals that there are four levels, or four "grades," of fruit-bearing that occurs. In verse two there is "no fruit" then in verse two; there is "fruit" or *some* fruit. Then, there is "more fruit," also in verse two. And finally, there is "much fruit" in verse five, and again in verse eight. So, the highest level of fruit-bearing is the "much fruit" level and in verse eight, Jesus said, "This is to my Father's glory, that you bear much fruit, showing yourselves to be my disciples." This is really frightening and at the same time fascinating to think about. We know that a Christian is dependent upon Christ, but this means that Jesus Christ is also dependent upon the Christian. Just like the vine depends on the branch to bear its fruit, so Jesus depends on the Christian to bear His fruit. Aurelius Augustine touched on this truth many centuries ago when he said, "Without Christ, we cannot, and without us, Christ will not." Remember, Christian, Jesus Christ is depending on you and me, and He is serious about it!

What is "fruit," anyway? Well, fruit is the result of overflowing life. When a branch receives all the sap or life necessary to meet its own needs, the extra life bursts forth in the form of fruit. Jesus Christ said in John 10:10, "I came that they may have life *(to cover their own needs)*, and that they might have it abundantly *(to communicate it to others)*" (NASB). One translation says, "And that they might have it with a surplus." The word "abundant" suggests an overflow. Our abiding in Christ leads to abounding for Christ. In 2 Corinthians 9:8, the Bible says that "God is able to make all grace abound *(overflow)* toward you, that you, always having all sufficiency in all things, may abound *(overflow)* in every good work."

That overflow of life is always for someone else! There it is again… that *others* thing. With many Christians, there is no fruit simply because there is no abounding, no fullness of life that causes an overflow. Fruit is simply overflowing life. Then fruit is the natural product of a healthy vine. You do not have to command a grapevine to bear grapes, or an apple tree to bear apples. If the plants are healthy, they naturally bear fruit after their own kind. Fruit-bearing is an effortless thing. When the branch abides in the vine, the natural product is fruit. It's a lot like the shining of a light bulb. There is a light bulb shining over my head as I write these words. I did not command that light bulb to shine. If the light bulb is in working order, it must be in its place and turned on, and then it will shine. If the believer is in her place in Christ and abiding there, and turned on (willing to be a conductor of the sap of the vine, the life of the Lord Jesus Christ), she will bear fruit. Fruit is natural.

Also, fruit has the flavor of the vine that it's a part of, and the Christian is to have the flavor of Jesus Christ in his life. Jesus Christ does not want you to work for Him; He wants you to let Him do His best through you. This is fruit—Jesus Christ producing His life and character and works in and through you. I am supposed to walk, talk and smell like Jesus.... And taste like Him too. What is fruit for, anyway? Who is it for? A vine does not eat its own fruit. It's always for others, others, others! Outward Christianity is Christ-like Christianity.

There are also several categories of fruit seen in the New Testament that a Christian should bear in abundance in their life. There is *character* fruit, the fruit that is mentioned in Galatians 5:22-23. Here, the character of Christ is revealed in a believer's life in some nine characteristics, three developed toward God the Father, three toward other people, and three toward the believer himself. Then there is *convert* fruit, or the Christian being used to produce other Christians. This fruit is suggested in John 15:16, where Jesus said, "You have not chosen me, but I have chosen you, and ordained you that you should go and bring forth fruit, and that your fruit should remain." Give special attention to the little word, "go." This is Christ's usual missionary word, His commission word. One does not need to go to bear the fruit of Christian character, but one must go to win other people to Christ.

Then there is *conduct* fruit, the kind of fruit we bear when Christ produces through us a conduct like His. Thus, our lives will be morally like His, and ministerially like His. This fruit is suggested in Colossians 1:10 and Philippians 1:11. Then, there is *contribution* fruit, which concerns the way a Christian gives and eternally invests his money and material resources. Read Philippians 4:13-19 and Romans 15:25-28 for good discussions of this kind of fruit.

And finally, there is *confessional* fruit, "the fruit of your lips giving thanks and praise to His Name" (Hebrews 13:15). This concerns the way in which a Christian should consistently use his daily speech to praise Jesus and bear testimony to Him. If a branch does not bear fruit, it is cheating and defrauding the husbandman. And if the Christian does not bear fruit, she is missing her most delightful destiny and is defrauding Jesus Christ. You see, by the fruit, which Christians bear, the world judges both the Vine and the Husbandman. The Christian is to bear fruit; this is the new product of the Christian life.

There really are so many new things that are mine as a Christian. Not only do I have a new position in Christ and a new possession in Christ, and a new product in life; I have a new *purpose* in life. My purpose and your purpose is defined in this passage in John fifteen by the one little word "abide." This word is used nine times in the first eleven verses and it expresses the total responsibility of the Christian life. In fact, there is just one command for you and I to obey in this entire text. Our total responsibility as Christians is to abide in Jesus Christ. This simply means that we are to keep the point of contact between us and Jesus Christ intact at all times. The most vital part of the branch is the small area where the vine and branch connect. The only real concern of the Christian is to be sure that she abides in Christ.

Beloved, we must stay zeroed-in or focused on Jesus Christ at all times, drawing the very vitality of our lives from Him. This means that we must use every possible means to keep the channel open between us, and the Lord Jesus.

Suppose you stood in a large room with me, and as I surveyed the room, I suddenly made a surprising announcement. "I'm going to fly around this room! If I can flap my arms a few minutes for a warm-up, I think I can get up enough ground speed running down one side of this room to get airborne, then I think I can make a few sharp turns—and I can fly around this room" I will promise you one thing: you would stay and watch! But we would both know that the outcome would be quite predictable: as I dived out in the air to be airborne, I would crash-land on my nose. You probably smile as you think about such foolishness, but be very careful. The very person you are smiling at—Cheri Holcomb—has flown over broad oceans. I had a lot of stops along the way because that much flapping of the arms made me awfully tired! Of course, you know what I did: I boarded an airplane, an incredibly complicated machine that is designed to fly, I put myself in the care of a person trained to fly it, and all I had to do was buckle my seat belt and abide. Whatever happened to the plane would happen to me—simply because I was in it.

When the Apostle John was summarizing the Christian life, he wrote in 1 John 2:28, "And now, little children, abide in Christ; that, when he shall appear, we may have confidence, and not be ashamed before him at His coming." The Christian, then, has a new purpose for his entire life—to abide in Christ. So you, dear one, have four new things since you became a Christian that you did not have before: You have a new position—in Christ; you have a new possession—Christ is in you; you have a new product—fruit unto God; and you have a new purpose— to abide in Christ.

Beloved, we need to be "hanging with Jesus" and the fruit will naturally make its way outward. May the Holy Spirit disclose to each of us the vast riches that are ours because we are new creatures in Christ.

So, what does your fruit look like, anyway?

Father, may we learn to abide, to nestle in close to your heart each day and find all we need there. You are our source of life. You are the reason we have life. May our lives bear you much fruit, and so prove to be your disciples. I ask it in Jesus mighty name because You said I could. Amen.

CHAPTER EIGHT

It All Adds Up…
A Ministry of
Multiplication

The things which you have heard from me in the
presence of many witnesses, entrust these to faithful men who will be able to teach others also.

—2 Timothy 2:2 NASB

Like so many, when I was saved I was immediately involved in every
facet of the church as well as being trained in all the dimensions of the
Christian life. We were at church every time the doors were open. We
served in any and every capacity they would allow us to. I have been
saved since June of 1975 and have taught Sunday school and Bible studies for almost 30 of my 34 years in Christ. I love church and I love the
family of God. I love people. I have always been a soul winner. I have
always had a burden for the lost. Even as a babe in Christ myself, I was
witnessing daily and seeing people saved almost weekly. I have had some
incredible witnessing opportunities.

One of the earliest soul winning experiences and still one of the highlights of my Christian walk was one evening in 1976. Lee and I were
driving home late that evening after Bible study and we passed a local
convenience store in a not-so-safe part of town, if you know what I mean!

I felt a strong compelling of the Holy Spirit to stop at that convenience store for a witness opportunity. It was about 10:30 at night and my husband, as you can well imagine, was not easily convinced that my compelling was from the Lord. But, I finally convinced him to stop so that I could see what God might have for me. Before Lee could even get out of the car, I asked him to just wait and I would be right back. As soon as I entered the store, I was immediately aware of a transaction taking place between a pimp and his prostitutes. It was another one of those Wow! moments. The two ladies gave this man their money and he turned towards me, walked right past me, almost brushing my shoulder, and yet never seemed to even notice me there. The two ladies looked at me with somewhat of a surprised look. I seized the moment! I said, "Listen; I know you might just think that I am crazy. But, God sent me in here to tell you that he has a plan for your life and this is not it!" I said, "Please come home with me and let me tell you about this man Jesus and how he saved my life and changed me on the inside." I tell you.... those girls did not even hesitate! It was as though God had already tilled up that soil so well that the seed I flung at them, just fell into well-prepared soil. They agreed to come with me if I would bring them back there later. Now, the best and perhaps even funny part of this story is the look on Lee's face when I came walking out of that store with these two ladies of the evening and told him that they were coming home with us. It was priceless!

When we got to our home, my sweet husband, the servant's heart that he has, went right into the kitchen and put on a pot of coffee. He knew we just might be awhile. I sat in our living room with these two ladies and began to share the gospel of Jesus Christ with them. I told them what Christ had done for me. Now, I was just a babe in Christ and some of their questions had me a little stumped. But, I knew where I could get help with leading these ladies to Christ and so I excused myself and went into the kitchen and phoned my pastor, Brother Herb Hodges. It was around midnight by now and when Herb answered his phone, he answered with a bit of concern as anyone would at that hour. But, that concern quickly turned to fright when I said, "Brother Herb, I have two prostitutes here." "What!" he exclaimed. I could only imagine what he thought. I continued, I am trying to win them to Jesus, Brother Herb, and I need your help!" Herb was at my house in a flash. Herb was always so available to his flock to help build them to be reproducers for Christ. Herb came in, he pulled off his shoes and sat down Indian style in the middle of the living room floor with me sitting right along side him willing to watch and learn. Herb so humbly answered their questions and encouraged me to take them through the Romans Road to salvation. I explained the Scriptures to them and shared how Christ had delivered Lee and me from a life of drugs and alcohol. It was a wow moment! Herb and I lead those two prostitutes to faith in Christ. With tears flowing down both their faces they prayed the sinner's prayer. Oh, the power of Jesus' name! What joy there is in seeing others come to Christ. I love to share my faith and see others come to know Christ. I am so thankful that God uses ordinary people to do His Kingdom's work. I could share hundreds of stories just like that one and am grateful for every opportunity to be used by God to fling the seed of the glorious gospel.

Even with all of these opportunities, I never dreamed that I could be falling short in regard to God's call upon my life. I have always been a woman of the Word. I was trained by it and I love God and His Word and desire to be found faithful. The study and memorization of the Scriptures has transformed my life more than anything else.

For the Word of God is living and active and sharper than any two-edged sword, and piercing as far as the division of soul and spirit, of both joints and marrow, and able to judge the thoughts and intentions of the heart. (Hebrews 4:12 NASB)

However, I have come to understand that there is still more to be done with a person than just leading that person to faith in Christ. Salvation is only the beginning. Jesus did not say, "Go and make good decent human beings. He did not say, go and make good church attendees. Jesus said, "Go and turn people into disciples." And disciples were and are re-producers!

We will never do anything more Christ-like than to "turn people into disciples" for Christ. These disciples are reproducers for Jesus Christ. Disciples are people who love the Lord and reach their world. I want to be a disciple maker, thus fulfilling my part in the Great Commission, the only mandate Christ gave to His church.

Go therefore and make disciples of all the nations, baptizing them in the name of the Father and the Son and the Holy Spirit, teaching them to observe all that I commanded you; and lo, I am with you always, even to the end of the age. (Matthew 28:19-20 NASB)

Several years ago, I committed my life to being just that, a disciple and disciple maker. I had to better understand what that really meant, so I started with much reading. I read several wonderful books on disciple making and was strongly encouraged and blessed by them all. But, there is one book in particular that changed everything for me. Herb's book, *Tally Ho, The Fox!* was the most life-changing and ministry-motivating book of all for me personally. Of course I'm biased. He is my Papaw after all! This study gave me the blueprint, the strategy that I needed to become a reproducer of reproducers. And this is what Christ expects.

I knew I needed to be involved in a ministry of multiplication or my personal ministry for Christ would fall short of His mandate for me.

I started with prayer, simply asking God to enlarge my capacity to know Him first personally and powerfully, so that I could have that necessary influence on someone else for Him. I want to live a life worth following. I prayed that Father would bring me at least one woman who would be at least teachable and faithful; a woman that I could pour my life into with a focused, systematic strategy. Basically, my strategy was to just flesh it out before her, teaching her by example first and then by curriculum. I was totally dependent upon God to do the work through me and I still believe this is the key to any successful ministry. I was totally dependent upon Jesus to bring me a disciple and to build that disciple through me. I personally have nothing to offer. All any of us has to offer really is our capacity to be filled and God must bring the supply. I was and am well aware that I am nothing and can do nothing apart from Him at work in and through me.

Within the first year, my Father brought four seminary wives across my path as a result of a Precept Bible study I was teaching at a local church in our area. All four of these young ladies seemed to be seeking to know Christ in a deeper way, and they seemed to have the necessary commitment to go through the process of disciple making. It sounds so technical, but it is really very practical. Jesus was an absolute genius! He took a small group of men and He poured Himself into them for three years. He taught them by example and He was their curriculum! All I needed to do was follow Jesus, closely imitating His example for disciple making.

So, I started a small group with these four ladies, meeting once a week in my home. "In my home" is very important. I have come to understand that disciple making is a life-on-life ministry and not another program of the local church. I cannot find in the Scriptures one place where

Jesus took his disciples to church. Jesus took them to *life* with him! Jesus did not see Zaccehus up in that tree one day and say, "Hey Zac, come on down and let's go to church." No, Jesus said, "come on down because I am going to your house today." This is a picture of getting in a life, not just a once-a-week acquaintance. I like to call it getting all up in your stuff! True ministry will cost us time and true ministry will cost us transparency. I live at home. The real me can be seen at my house. Amen? It is important for women to see who we truly are and how we live and flesh out this faith in real life.

Another part of the building of a disciple-making strategy is Scripture memory. I created a list; a Scripture memory challenge with over sixty five passages of Scriptures for my ladies to memorize. All of which seemed to be practical in their application. I believe this is necessary for being a Christ-centered believer. This Scripture memory was and still is an absolute priority and the prerequisite for any woman that I disciple personally.

I ask my disciples for a one-year commitment or longer if needed to make the necessary spiritual deposits into their lives, striving to assure a ministry of multiplication through such deposits. My ultimate goal is to see every women set out on her own course of reproduction through the very same standard, using the very same curriculum that I have taught her, thus modeling the standard found in 2 Timothy 2:2. This is a concentrated deposit of spiritual truths and principles as well as the daily disciplines of the faith necessary to produce a world-impacting reproducer for Jesus Christ. These disciplines include a regular daily quiet time, an ever-deepening prayer life, and boldness in their personal soul-winning and hiding God's Word regularly in her heart. But I truly believe that these vital principles are more caught than they are taught.

Bonnie Everly, one of my "primary Timothias" is a wonderful example of the standard taking root and changing a person's entire life and ministry. She is one who surely caught this vision and the passion for a ministry of multiplication. Bonnie came to me, a retired flight attendant, with plenty of free time and I took full advantage of it. I took Bonnie everywhere with me, and I still do! We pray together daily and Bonnie has learned to be a bold faithful witness by seeing it modeled for her. This is just vital, people! This is a woman who was fully engaged in all of the church activities and found herself "in captivity to activity," spinning her spiritual wheels but making no real headway for Christ and His Kingdom's work. She was a Sunday school teacher and the founder and leader of a women's ministry, even on the Pastor's prayer team; and still felt strangely unfulfilled. Bonnie, like many Christians, realized that something vital was still missing in her Christian life, even though she was so busy for God. There was still that illusive something missing. That something was *intimacy with* God rather than being *busy for* God. I laid out the prerequisite for disciple making and she hit the ground running. Bonnie had never been taught how to cultivate a quiet time but learned very quickly the powerful result of this basic discipline in a believer's life. She has learned to be a bold witness and a woman of the Word. She learned the value of memorizing the Scripture and her prayer life has deepened more than she ever thought possible.

In February of 2005, Bonnie and I went on our first mission trip together to El Salvador with the Benny Jackson Evangelistic Association. I can remember her excitement as we went out into the streets of the city of San Salvador each day flinging the seed of the gospel. Bonnie was so eager to be a soul winner and this was just fuel for my own passion to win the lost. Our days were spent ministering and praying for the sick and always sharing the gospel of Jesus Christ with anyone and everyone who would listen. In the evenings we participated in worship services and God was moving mightily among us.

One evening during the worship service, I noticed that the streets outside the church were full of people. So many had come and could not find room inside and some were even too afraid to enter and would stand at a distance and observe. Every one of the locals were seemingly captivated by what they saw and heard inside. Perhaps some of the excitement was the curiosity for these "gringos" who were among them. But whatever it was, the street was full of people, and I knew this would be a wonderful opportunity to teach Bonnie the power of prayer and a bold witness. I took Bonnie by the hand and led her through the crowds into the street outside and turned to her and said, "You hold on to me and just watch and pray." I turned and immediately spotted a young man by the name of Gabriel. I had tried to witness to Gabriel earlier in the day while up in the mountains with my translator, a curious man by the name of Oscar. Bonnie had not been with me earlier on that mission but I had told her about Gabriel.

I had seen Gabriel several times throughout that day standing at a distance just watching as I would talk with the locals and share my faith in Christ. I had even asked Oscar who this man was and all Oscar would say is, "He a very bad man." He told me that the people in the village were very afraid of Gabriel. So, obviously there was something in this man's past that made him less attractive as a witness for Oscar. But, I told Oscar that we simply must go and tell Gabriel about Jesus. As we walked over to Gabriel, he began to move away and Oscar told him not to run but that the gringo (me) had something very important to tell him. As I approached him I began to tell him of Christ's great love and sacrifice for him on the cross. I told him that Jesus had saved me from a destructive life of alcohol and drug abuse and that he wanted to save him as well. But every time I would ask Gabriel if he too would like to receive Christ, he would say something in Spanish and Oscar would not tell me what the man was saying. After a few times of trying to reach this man with the gospel, we left and returned to the church.

Now, here this young man is standing in the street outside the church listening to the gospel being preached. My heart just jumped, because I knew that our heavenly Father had drawn him there by my witness earlier that day. With Bonnie standing behind me, our hands clutched together, I began again to plead with Gabriel to give his heart to Christ and Bonnie prayed. And again, he would resist, saying much more than Oscar was willing to interpret for me. I looked at Oscar and said, "God is moving here Oscar, what is Gabriel trying to tell me? It's okay Oscar, we don't have to be afraid." Oscar turned to me and said, "Ms., He says that he has killed many people. He says that he has no heart and that your God cannot save him."

I began to weep. I told Oscar and Bonnie to just pray and pray hard! I felt the Holy Spirit telling me to kneel down in front of Gabriel and look up into his eyes. I obeyed. I knew that others were watching and surely wouldn't understand and probably not approve. But, I knew Father had given me instruction and I was going to obey for the sake of the gospel. I looked into that young man's eyes and with tears rolling down my face I told him that God's love could reach down even through all of his great sin and save him. I told him that God could and would give him a new heart if he would only pray, turn from all of his sin and trust Christ as Savior and Lord. You could just feel the power of the Holy Spirit moving.

As I was telling Gabriel that Jesus would come inside of him and would make him a new man—all of a sudden he began to shout and with an obvious change of expression upon his face. A slew of words flooded out of that man that made me shiver. I asked, "Oscar, what is he saying?" Oscar with tears as well said, "He wants to be saved, he wants to saved right now." I began to share Romans 10:9-10, That if you confess with your mouth, "Jesus is Lord," and believe in your heart that God raised him from the dead, you will be saved. For it is with your heart that you believe and are justified, and it is with your mouth that you confess and are saved."

So, I led Gabriel through the Romans Road and the sinner's prayer and he was gloriously saved that night! Bonnie was so excited. She shared with me afterwards that at the very moment I began to share Romans 10:9-10 that she was thinking of that very passage and praying that I would share it with Gabriel. How wonderful it is to see the Holy Spirit at work in our hearts as we pray and fling the seed of the gospel of Jesus Christ. Wow…we were so overjoyed to have been a part of what God was doing in that place. There is such power in partnering for the gospel sake. The power of training and building others in the essentials of the faith by modeling it for them is just incredible. This stuff works!

We looked around again to see who we might share Christ with and saw five teenage boys standing across the street watching everything that had just taken place. They were giggling and obviously very mischievous boys. Bonnie and I still hand in hand, and Oscar by our side walked right over to them and I said, "You boys have been hearing this preaching of God's Word, and you have seen this man give his heart to Christ. You had better understand the seriousness of this gospel that you are making fun of. God doesn't take lightly to you laughing at Him." I tell you the Spirit of God was obviously moving and two of the boys immediately began to tear up and said, "We want to be saved, please can we be saved?" After the two of them prayed to receive Christ, one of the others surrendered as well. It was absolutely glorious!

There are so many stories that can be told of all God did while we were there in El Salvador. I will testify to this: our God still delivers the demon possessed! He still heals the leper! He still resurrects all kinds of dead things! I have seen God resurrect dead marriages! He still calms the storms and provides mighty walls of protection from the serpent's bite or the poisonous drink. All for those who would walk by faith always going, seeking to make disciples of all nations, thus fulfilling the mandate to go and make disciples of all the nations; all in the power of and the name of Jesus Christ.

Bonnie is now a multi-generational disciple maker herself and has become a faithful ministry partner with In The Cross-Ties Discipleship Ministries. She travels all over the world with me teaching and training women how to come to their fullest potential in Christ through this Great Commission lifestyle of disciple making. I thank God for her and so many women like her that have come through this process of disciple making with me. I have been changed through the process as much as they themselves.

I have been so humbled and amazed at the ground covered in these past six years. I started just six years ago with this strategy and a systematic curriculum, expecting that woman to turn by faith and to make that same exact deposit into the life of that next available woman. In six years, I have been blessed with a multi-generational downline that far exceeds my wildest expectations. The simple truth is "this stuff works!" This is His method. Jesus saw the masses through the man and then He built the man to reach the masses, instead of the typical church mentality which is to cultivate a "seeker, sit and soak" body of believers that have no more clout after fifty years of salvation than the day they were saved. God help us!

One of the most humbling and rewarding experiences I have ever had is when I was on a flight to Atlanta, Georgia. Several years ago a woman came up to me shortly after the plane took off and asked, "Are you Cheri Holcomb?" I said, "Yes, do I know you?" She said, "No, you don't know me, but I am your great, great granddaughter in Jesus." That precious child of God went on to tell me about the woman I had won to Christ and discipled, and she was now discipling her. I was brought to tears!

The incredible endearing relationships that are built through this kind of lifestyle are just beyond comparison or explanation. God has brought massive numbers of women into my life and all are so precious to me. Some have passed through on their way to mission fields on the other side of the world. Two specific women that have left their own mark on my life and ministry are Marie Adioye and Marie Simeon. Marie Adioye is from Cote D'Ivoire, also known as the Ivory Coast in West Africa. Marie Simeon is from Haiti. Both of these precious women are the wives of two incredible men of God. They were here in the United States for their Christian education at Mid-America Baptist Theological Seminary in Memphis. I had been meeting with these two ladies for several months and God was blessing us with insight and absolutely captivating our hearts with a world vision.

One day as I was walking these two precious sisters to the door after our study time; Marie Adioye turned to me with tears in her eyes and said in her wonderful broken English: "Mama, you will reach Africa from here in your living room." It just hit us! As I pour this strategy into her, she will return home to West Africa trained, built, equipped to reproduce the very same thing in the lives of the women there, thus fulfilling her part in the Great Commission. It was a big Wow! moment for both of us. We were moved to tears with the thought of standing together at God's throne one day knowing that our labor was not in vain and Africa will stand there as a testimony. The lights had been turned on and forever turned on. Beloved, once you see this, you cannot un-see it! We can reach the world for Christ and we can do it from our own living rooms.

Revelation chapter five has always been one of my favorite passages of Scripture; verses nine through thirteen in particular. Just think beloved, one day, we will all stand before God's throne, and there will be a great multitude of people, from every tribe and every tongue and every nation. I want to know that my life and ministry recruited for Christ, many of those from around the world.

And they sung a new song, saying, "Thou art worthy to take the book, and to open the seals thereof: **for thou wast slain, and hast redeemed us to God by thy blood out of every kindred, and tongue, and people, and nation;** And hast made us unto our God kings and priests: and we shall reign on the earth." And I beheld, and I heard the voice of many angels round about the throne and the beasts and the elders: and the number of them was ten thousand times ten thousand, and thousands of thousands; Saying with a loud voice, "Worthy is the Lamb that was slain to receive power, and riches, and wisdom, and strength, and honour, and glory, and blessing." And every creature which is in heaven, and on the earth, and under the earth, and such as are in the sea, and all that are in them, heard I saying, "Blessing, and honour, and glory, and power, be unto him that sitteth upon the throne, and unto the Lamb for ever and ever." (KJV)

I realized for the first time that on that day, when we stand before the throne of God, I will look around me and from the tribes of Africa I will see my own grandchildren through Marie Adioye and this awesome ministry of spiritual multiplication.

In disciple making it often becomes a two-way ministry; I disciple them and they also disciple me. This was true of the Apostle Paul and Dr. Luke. It is easy to see how truly incredible God's plan for world impact is. We need one another to get the job done. I am so thankful for all of the precious women Father has brought into my life. I also realize my own personal benefit and spiritual growth gained because of the faithfulness and single heartedness of these precious women. The many friendships and partnerships for the gospel and for women's ministry are just amazing and truly humbling. You Timothias know exactly who you are and I pray that you will come to understand one day the deep love and respect I have for each one of you as I watch you pursue God's mandate for your life, to go…and make disciples!

Beloved, stay in His presence, keep your feet and your heart turned "outward" toward a lost and dying world. And if Jesus comes back today, I will see each of you over there in New Jerusalem! There is only one way to get there. "Neither is there salvation in any other: for there is none other name under heaven given among men, whereby we must be saved" (Acts 4:12 KJV).

CHAPTER NINE

Multiplied Lives

As I have shared in this book, many people have helped to shape my life as a disciple of Christ and a disciple maker. What better way to end this book than with stories from some of those who have truly caught the vision for world impact through this Great Commission lifestyle. I have seen first hand the genius of Christ's strategy to build world-impacting disciples and am confident through these precious women, that this process will continue until Jesus comes. May you be blessed as you read how God is working in these womens' lives—and may you be encouraged through their stories to make your own spiritual investments into the lives of others, to secure a ministry of multiplication through disciple making.

Biblical disciple making has taught me what true intimacy with my Savior feels like as Christ is being "fully formed" in me. (Galatians 4:19). I deem it an honor to have been discipled by one who has caught the vision for world impact for Christ, and make it my aim to follow that example by finishing my course well. The two disciplines of disciple making that have transformed my life the most are prayer and Scripture memorization. I've learned to "come with boldness to the throne of grace to obtain mercy and find grace" and "I stand on the ramparts to see what the Lord will speak to me." And hiding God's Word in my heart has given me that boldness as I pray His Own Will, armed with His Own Word. While being discipled, I was able to memorize over 65 passages of Scripture in three months, and I can testify that God's Word really is living and active and powerful against the enemy.

Making disciples involves a deep and timely investment into the lives of others but has become the greatest joy of my life. The words of this poem explain how I have seen Cheri's life modeled and I now make it my daily prayer:

Employ me in Thy service, Lord
And train me for Thy Will
And I will seek for no reward
Except to serve Thee still.

Imagine what the world would be like if every believer had a similar testimony, of becoming world-visionary, world-impacting, multiplying, reproducers to the ends of the earth till the end of time! I thank, Cheri, my dear "Paulette," for investing her time and life in me so I can invest His life in others.

—Bonnie Everly, Collierville, Tennessee

I have been saved since I was a little girl (over 40 years) and nothing has affected my spiritual life as much as learning to be a true disciple of Christ and a disciple maker, as the Master was. Cheri was the guest speaker at my church and she spoke on disciple making. I was unable to attend but some of the ladies invited me to attend a once-a-month class that Cheri was teaching. I was challenged by Cheri's lessons and quickly realized my own need to be discipled. I began the process with Bonnie Everly, one of Cheri's disciples and was hooked! It has been about six months now and the Lord has moved mightily in my life. Memorizing the Scriptures has had the greatest effect on my spiritual life. For the first time I am understanding, more fully, the tools and strategy that our Lord gave us. It is being modeled before me by Bonnie each week. She is laying down her life, giving up her agenda and teaching us how to be disciple makers. "Greater love hath no man than this that a man lay down his life for his friends" (John 15:13).

I am now being equipped to lead other ladies in the same process. I now have a group of ladies that I disciple weekly. I have even begun a one-on-one discipling with a new Christian who had been living on the streets. God has revealed to me in His Word how to stop the revolving door complex in our churches, but it takes sacrifice. I can now see how one little Christian like me, can stem the flow of mere "pew sitting" Christianity by learning and teaching Christ's message of total world impact. He came to save that which was lost and He calls us to be fishers of men and He did not leave us without instructions on how to do this. I am only at the beginning of this journey and can't wait to see what God will do in and through me, and through others, as we win the world for Christ!

—Annette Hull, Millington, Tennessee

A few years ago, I was blessed to serve on a mission trip with a godly woman who is obedient to Jesus and His command in the Great Commission in Matthew 28:19-20. She was willing to entrust His truths to me and to sacrifice whatever it took for my benefit, so that I was standing firm in my faith and being obedient to His command to "go and make disciples of all nations…" I've spent the last four years weekly in her home, as she pours into me the love of Christ and *His* strategy for building disciples. She would prefer to remain anonymous, and I love Cheri for that because it isn't about her—but, I thank God daily for her, and for her obedience to Him. I'm overwhelmed that she agreed to disciple me. I want to be just like Jesus, who is so evident in her, that when people see me they have to ask, "What is it about you? Something's different. You've changed." And, I'll take the opportunity to tell them just what it is that's different, and just Who it was that changed me, and how the disciple-maker's strategy really works. My life has been forever changed. I have been given a miracle of spiritual illumination, and now I *see* what God has on His heart and that's to reach a lost and dying world through the spreading of Christ's aroma everywhere.

This is what is now on my heart… I've been given the strategy to walk, talk and smell more like Jesus.

He is the image of the invisible God, the firstborn over all creation; for by Him, all things were created; things in heaven and on earth, visible and invisible, whether thrones or powers or rulers or authorities; all things were created by Him and for Him. He is before all things, and, in Him, all things hold together… He has reconciled you through His death, to present you holy in His sight, without blemish and free from accusation—if you continue in your faith, established and firm, not moved from the hope held out in the gospel (Colossians 1:15-17; 22-23).

—Melissa Armstrong, Somerville, Tennessee

A page from a pastor's wife's journal May 7, 2009: Father, I pray today that you would enlighten me through your Word. God, I have been praying that I would find my passion for you again. I realize and ask forgiveness for my neglect in reading and studying your Word. I've been too busy to spend time with you, Lord; you are so good to me. Yet because I have been so discouraged and frustrated with church, I just quit—I know you have never left me but I feel so alone in my walk. I have always had others to encourage me and to fellowship with, but I've been doing this all on my own for a while. Honestly, I am empty! Please forgive me. I don't even know what to pray, but you know my heart. Thank you for allowing me to go with Cheri the other night and hear Your voice speak to me. How am I supposed to minister to others when I am not full myself? I don't know what my future holds but I know You hold my future. Help me to be obedient, bold, courageous and compassionate where needed. Guide me in your truth! Use me for your glory— in spite of me! I love you Jesus! Amen.

July 22, 2009, five weeks after beginning the disciple-making process: I have been a Christian now for twenty seven years and have been in ministry with my husband for four years. I have seen God do amazing things in my life. I have had many spiritual markers along the way. I have taken Bible studies, been involved in accountability groups, gone to many conferences, but nothing has changed my view of my walk with Jesus until I became involved in the disciple-making process. I have truly been challenged to see the world through God's eyes and see His people the way He sees them. I have realized the importance of His Word and hiding it in my heart, and spending time alone with Him every day. The biggest difference right now has been the realization that my salvation is not about me, and no matter how much I feed myself, it is not until I pour that out into someone else with the intentions of making disciples, can Jesus truly be manifested in me. It is not good enough to be a better Christian but do nothing with that for the sake of others. God's intention for us was to first become a disciple, and then to reproduce that in others. I now look at the circle of influence I have as an opportunity for me to disciple other women the way I am being discipled. God's vision is not just for the people we surround ourselves with but for us to reach the whole world, and the way to do that is one disciple at a time. I can't help but think of what would have happened if the twelve that Jesus chose decided to just keep the gospel for themselves. I now have a new passion for Christ and for his people. I want to be obedient to live my life worthy of the calling He has put on my life by fulfilling the Great Commission. I am so thankful for godly men and women who are willing to rise up and invest their lives in others for the sake of His Kingdom. I am so grateful God has shown me the importance and responsibility of being His disciple and I look forward to those He may send to me for this very same process.

—Melinda Carlisle, Olive Branch Mississippi

The strategy of Jesus has completely revolutionized my life. I went from a faithful, church-going, pew potato, auditing Christian to a dynamic individual with the goal of reaching the entire world for Jesus Christ. For years I dedicated myself to church programs and church work. I remember a time when I was at the church six out of seven nights a week working *for* God. I remember being so tired then. I was tired of working so hard with hardly any support from other believers and hardly any results within the lost world. Then one day, Jesus stepped in. Praise His Name! I was introduced to the true strategy of Jesus. For years I had tried to come up with my own strategy—a new way to reach people. Yet, it had already been developed for me 2,000 years before. I was introduced by a Spirit-walking disciple maker, to the marching orders of the Great Commission: an order that is completely encompassed in the words "make disciples." My intimacy with Jesus has been revolutionized, because now I know how to cultivate a relationship with Him. My motivation with the gospel has been energized, because now I know how to spread it with confidence. My vision has been completely changed, and now I see the world through His eyes. I no longer work *for* God, I work *with* God. By following His strategy of seeing the masses through the man and building the man to impact the masses, for the first time in my life I can truly see the Savior moving and reaching the world around me. He has placed His stamp of approval on this strategy, because it is truly a continuation of what He began over 2,000 years ago.

—Melissa Petermann, Memphis, Tennessee

I accepted Christ as my Savior in my twenties and got busy in the church. If the doors were open most likely I was there. But when difficult times came I realized that the "get'em saved get'em busy" motto did not work. As a single I had sat under Cheri's teaching and when the tough times came I turned to her. It was then I began to sit under her teaching once a week for a year. In that time the group I was in learned how to walk, talk and smell like Jesus, how to pray corporately, how to be open and honest about our struggles, and how to memorize *a lot* of Scripture. We learned to see people through God's eyes and that where there is no vision people perish. That we need to get in on the greatest process we could ever imagine and that is teaching others what we have been taught so that they can teach others also—the process of multiplication. Without multiplication the Word of life and truth will not continue.

Since my time with Cheri I have discipled two young ladies, have gotten married, had a child and moved to North Carolina. As we get more and more involved in our new church we are seeing the need for disciple making. I feel equipped to make disciples! My husband is passing the bread basket as he teaches our Sunday School class and I will soon begin hosting a group of ladies and hope to pour my life into theirs just as Cheri poured hers into mine.

—Amy Bright, Hendersonville, North Carolina

About six years ago the Lord began stirring my heart but I just was uncertain as to what it exactly was. I was director of women's ministry at my church and knew there was something more than what we were offering and doing as women in Christ. I attended a leadership conference with other women who were serving in the ministry and consistently heard some of the same stirring. What was God up to? I still was not sure but continued to seek after it. Then one day I met with a woman (and yes, that woman was Cheri Holcomb) and before our time was over I knew my search was over. God has an anointing upon Cheri's life and I was drawn to what Christ was doing in and through her. I knew God wanted to be up to something big not only in my life but the lives of other women. Looking back on that time, I just did not realize what an eye-opening (illumination!) experience I was in for while discovering what I had been missing for all these years.

Cheri began discipling me in her home along with several other women on a weekly basis. Through this disciple-making process, I began to truly understand what it meant to live the abundant Christian life. It had been about 25 years since I gave my life to Jesus Christ but I did not realize how much I was missing. For you see, I faithfully attended church three times a week, was active in Christian service, tithing and attending regular Bible studies. How could I have missed all these years the very thing the Lord taught me through disciple making? I don't know but all I can say now is *"Glory Hallelujah, I'm thrilled I've seen it now!"* Because once you have seen something you can't "un-see" it. But believe me, I don't want to!

Through disciple making I've learned so much as I watched it being lived out through Cheri's life. I'll share just a few highlights with you. After seeing it modeled I understood what it meant to totally surrender my life to His Lordship and receive the fullness of the Spirit. Next I knew I must continually be growing so I will enlarge my capacity to receive even more. Then bearing fruit began to come naturally. Not just being productive and busy for the Lord because once you have on your heart what is on the Father's heart then your purpose changes. What does the Father have on His heart? *People!* I have a responsibility to *"reproduce reproducers"* for the Kingdom of God like Paul told Timothy in 2 Timothy 2:2. I do not produce the fruit but I bear it when I am totally surrendered to Him. When this happens then the fruit I bear becomes automatic and of like-kind. Grape vines do not produce apples; nor does the grape vine have to be told to produce the grapes because it should occur automatically when it is abiding in the vine.

My prayer is that through the words Cheri has written—and even these words—you will begin to see things from God's point of view. But I must warn you once you begin to 'see' it, your life will never be the same! Exalted be His name forever and ever.

—Martha Tisdale, Collierville, Tennessee

Disciple making is all about life-transference, similar to birthing a child. When each of my sons were born, they were initially totally dependent on us to provide nourishment in every imaginable aspect. Yet with loving care, and over an expanse of time, our helpless sons progressed to being able to care for themselves and gradually to apply and pass on to their children what they had seen in our lives. Far too often we forget how significant this is spiritually. When I yielded my life to Christ, I was "hungry" for God's words. I needed a lot of guidance along the way because at this point I was a spiritual babe. People make professions of faith all the time, but if they lack a disciple maker to lead them into a deeper, more personal relationship with our Lord and Savior, they often drift away within a matter of weeks or months.

Disciple making is not a program that I attend for an hour or so once or twice a week—it is a 24-hour way of living as I try to become more and more like Jesus in my thoughts and actions. This is a total paradigm shift! Isaiah 55:8-9 reveals, "My thoughts are nothing like your thoughts," says the Lord. "And my ways are far beyond anything you could imagine. For just as the heavens are higher than the earth, so my ways are higher than your ways and my thoughts higher than your thoughts."

God has taught me that He does not expect me to be another Cheri Holcomb! But He does expect me to be the very best Leafa Miller I can be under His leadership. Even as Peter progressed from being Simon to Simon Peter to Peter (the Rock), Christ is using those disciple makers He has brought into my life to enable that transformation from sinner, to saved sinner, to the Leafa He knows I can be. These disciple makers have inspired me as they modeled application. Life doesn't happen in a vacuum—we need others to guide our growth and we must also share with others what we have learned.

Disciple making has taught me that knowledge alone will not empower others to be mature disciples of Christ. To have the greatest impact on those I am surrounded with, they must see transferable life application from the Scriptures as I live them out personally. As a genuine disciple maker I must have integrity in my life. This means being undivided between what I believe and how I live and think in front of people. It is consistently running the race Jesus set before me, whether other people are around or not.

God is continuing to transform this weak, immature, extremely introverted, no-self-esteem individual, so I know God can change your life too, *if* you will submit to someone spiritually more mature. Keep in mind that this disciple must not only disciple you, but must also be one who imparts the life-giving power of Christ in her life! *Then* you have the responsibility to pass it on, enabling disciple making to multiply until we have reached every person with God's Word. What an exciting journey I am on! Believe me, life does not have to be an enigma. I am alive because I have a vital relationship with Christ. I am learning everyday to trust Christ more completely as I talk with God and study His Word. And as Simon Peter … I stumble more than I should… but I will never quit until God welcomes me home.

—Leafa M. Miller, Marquette, Michigan

Discipleship and what it means to me is really very simple. It is the outward commitment of a heart that has been radically changed by the love of Christ Jesus. When I was in college I met Cheri, who was head over heels in love with Jesus. I had known about Him for a long time, but she really loved Him in a way that made me want to know what it was that she was so in love with Him about. She invited me into her home and daily we would meet to study His Word and pray. She would have me memorize Scripture. I just knew that was going to be a cinch, since I had been taught to do so as a child...John 3:16..., but not so much! My first assignment was Philippians 2:5-11. She was *serious* about knowing His Word. And I am so glad she was, because it was His Word that led me to Christ Jesus.

You see, disciple making was the process that the Holy Spirit used to draw me to the Word. The Word was the method. The Word says, "Faith cometh by hearing, and hearing by the Word of God." This is what Father God used to bring me to faith in Jesus Christ. The more I have studied and memorized the Word of God, the less effective the enemy and my flesh have been. John 8:31 says, "Then said Jesus to those Jews which believed on him, If ye continue in my word, then are ye my disciples indeed." So the part of discipleship that I cherish the most is His Word in my heart. The relationships that He brings through discipleship are products of the outward commitment of His Love in my life. It is Jesus who told us to make disciples, it is Jesus who is the Word, it is Jesus who is the Love, and it is Jesus who is Faithful. Therefore, discipleship is simply all about Jesus, ".... Him who fills all in all."

—Dara Pearman, Valdosta, Georgia

The disciple-making process has impacted my life in so many ways. My discipler poured what had been poured into her life, into me. I witnessed first hand the way disciple making had changed her life and wanted the same spiritual depth in my own life. My intimacy with Jesus Christ grew more precious to me as I was challenged to spend time daily in His Word and in prayer. I had been taught these disciplines of the faith and had practiced them sporadically. However, it was only as I was held accountable each week that I began to look forward to my time with God each morning. I began to cultivate a romance with my Savior and Lord. The fellowship of women gathering in homes is an added blessing. Our conversations are always focused on Jesus and His will and work in our lives. It just doesn't get any better than that!

—Tanya Moore, Somerville, Tennessee

I have had many struggles in my life. I married very young and lived through physical and emotional abuse for many years until that marriage finally ended in divorce. I remarried a wonderful man but somehow happiness and peace still eluded me. After recovering from a life-threatening car accident my life just continued to spiral downward, until I found myself very addicted to gambling at the local casinos.

In 2007, I attended the funeral of an ex-brother-in-law and heard Cheri deliver the eulogy for her cousin. She spoke about Jesus Christ and His great love and forgiveness; about having peace with God through Jesus. She had such a glow about her and as she spoke, I felt as though she were speaking directly to me. After the service ended, we spoke briefly and Cheri shared with me how I too, could have this peace through Jesus Christ and that it was free. I was so moved by her message but left that day still empty and longing for that peace she spoke of.

It was a year later that I phoned Cheri to inquire about a Bible study. I was so miserable and thought that perhaps a Bible study would help me out of my depression. She invited me to her home that next week and we sat and talked about life and the reality of sin and the cross and my need for salvation. God moved in my heart that day and sitting there at Cheri's kitchen table, I repented of my sin and asked Jesus to come into my heart and into my life. I was gloriously born again and I have never looked back! God filled me with such love and joy, and He totally delivered me that day from my gambling addiction. I began the disciple-making process the following week in Cheri's home and have been forever changed! I am confident that had I not been immediately discipled, I would have returned to the only life I knew. But, I now have Christian friends to love and to support me. It has been two years, and I now have four disciples that meet in my home weekly. I now am making those same spiritual deposits into their lives that were made in mine. I am so thankful to all of the ladies that have helped to disciple me.

—Carolyn Beasley, Hernando, Mississippi

Conclusion

I was only fifteen when I married and already had a full blown addiction to drugs and to alcohol. My life was full of sin and self. I was truly miserable and spiraling out of control, when someone shared the gospel of Jesus Christ with me. God began to deal with my hardened heart and on Sunday, June 1, 1975, sitting in a bathro-om at a friend's apartment; I prayed and asked the Lord Jesus to forgive me of my sin and to save me. Bless God, He did! I was gloriously born again and totally delivered from the strongholds in my life. I was immediately taken under the wing of a wonderful older woman who poured her own life into me. I learned from her the true way to follow Jesus through the biblical standard of disciple making. That process set in motion for me, the pursuit of leaving my own mark, my spiritual legacy for the glory of God. Disciple making is the very genius of Christ's strategy for reaching the world with the gospel, and I will do this as long as live. I believe with all of my heart that the heaven that awaits me is determined by those who are behind me.

In The Cross-Ties Ministries

Cheri Holcomb is founder of *In The Cross-Ties Discipleship Ministries*. She is a multi-generational disciple maker; a dynamic conference speaker as well as radio personality for WTNE 97.7 Grace Broadcasting Network, Jackson, Tennessee. Her ministry is committed to building the lives of generational multipliers through teaching and training in the biblical principles of disciple making according to the Great Commission of Matthew 28:19-20. Leading disciple-making conferences all over the United States reaching the international regions of Africa, El Salvador and Mexico; she shares with an infectious passion the transforming power of God in and through the life of ordinary people.

Cheri and her husband Lee are residents of Olive Branch, Mississippi and active members of a local fellowship there. She married in 1972 at the age of 15 and was saved in June of 1975 from a destructive life of drug and alcohol abuse. Through laughter and practical applications from the Word of God, Cheri challenges women all over the world to come to their fullest potential in Jesus Christ through the Great Commission lifestyle of disciple making.

For more information or to schedule a conference or retreats contact Cheri at inthecrossties@hotmail.com. A portion of all proceeds from conferences and retreats are reinvested for the training of other world impacting, reproducing disciples of Jesus Christ. We are a tax exempt 501c3 ministry.